Workshop on Computational Linguistics and Writing: Writing Processes and Authoring Aids 2010

Held at NAACL HLT 2010

Los Angeles, California, USA
6 June 2010

ISBN: 978-1-61738-673-2

Printed from e-media with permission by:

Curran Associates, Inc.
57 Morehouse Lane
Red Hook, NY 12571

Some format issues inherent in the e-media version may also appear in this print version.

Printed by Curran Associates, Inc. (2010)

For permission requests, please contact the Association for Computational Linguistics at the address below.

Association for Computational Linguistics
209 N. Eighth Street
Stroudsburg, Pennsylvania 18360

Phone: 1-570-476-8006
Fax: 1-570-476-0860

acl@aclweb.org

Additional copies of this publication are available from:

Curran Associates, Inc.
57 Morehouse Lane
Red Hook, NY 12571 USA
Phone: 845-758-0400
Fax: 845-758-2634
Email: curran@proceedings.com
Web: www.proceedings.com

Introduction

Writing today, whether professional, academic, or private, relies heavily on computers. Most texts composed in the 21st century are probably written on computers or other electronic devices, such as mobile phones. People compose texts in word processors, text editors, content management systems, blogs, wikis, e-mail clients, and instant messaging applications. Each of these tools supports authors in different ways and to different degrees.

Writing research has been concerned with word processing since the 1970s. Writing researchers today investigate specific characteristics of writing with computers and the effect of tools on writing processes. The current rise of new writing environments and genres (e.g., blogging) has prompted new studies in this area of research.

During the last few decades, computational linguistics has mostly been concerned with static or finished texts. We believe there is now a growing need to explore how computational linguistics can support human text production and word processing. However, there are still very few projects where computational linguists and writing researchers work together here.

The Workshop on Computational Linguistics and Writing (CL&W 2010) provides an overview of current developments in the area of computational linguistics for authoring aids, and an overview of recent advances in writing research. CL&W 2010 continues and builds on the workshops on authoring aids at the Sixth International Conference on Language Resources and Evaluation (LREC 2008) and the 2008 Swedish Language Technology Conference (SLTC 2008). The papers included here present research that explores writing processes and text production, as well as actual systems that support writers. In both areas, research on all languages is relevant, including less-resourced languages. CL&W 2010 brings together researchers from both communities, to identify areas where computational linguistics and writing research can benefit from each other and to stimulate discussion and interdisciplinary cooperation between these two areas of research.

In our call for papers we posed some questions:

- How can writing be supported by methods, resources, and tools from computational linguistics? This includes NLP tools and techniques that can be used or have been used to support writing (e.g., grammar and style checking, document structuring, thematic segmentation, and editing and revision aids).
- How can we gain a better understanding of writing processes, strategies, and needs? How can techniques from HCI research and psychology help us to gain new insights into the composition and writing processes, and to improve writing tools?
- Which methods, resources, and tools from computational linguistics might support research in this area?
- How do high-level writing processes and the mechanics of writing relate to each other?
- How does the tool used influence composition (including editing and revising)? Are writers aware of the possibilities and limitations of their writing tools?

- Is there a need for the development of new writing tools? What can we learn from earlier approaches and tools like RUSKIN, Writer's Workbench, or Augment, or from source code editors for programming languages?
- How can insights from writing research and methods from computational linguistics help to support the needs of particular user groups (e.g., foreign language learners, children, persons with disabilities)?

We received 15 submissions from both computational linguists and writing researchers. After a rigorous review process we selected 9 papers for the workshop. We would like to thank the members of the Program Committee for their excellent work—the reviews were all very thorough, carefully written, detailed, and helped the authors to improve their papers.

The papers cover a variety of topics, ranging from actually working—and freely available!—systems to support novice and expert authors, to more general thoughts on the intersection of writing research and computational linguistics. We are pleased to present these papers in this volume.

We hope the work presented here will trigger discussion and collaboration between researchers, bringing together expertise and interest from writing research and computational linguistics.

Michael Piotrowski, Cerstin Mahlow, and Robert Dale

Organizers:

Michael Piotrowski, University of Zurich (Switzerland)
Cerstin Mahlow, University of Zurich (Switzerland)
Robert Dale, Macquarie University (Australia)

Program Committee:

Gerd Bräuer, Zurich University of Applied Sciences (Switzerland)
Jill Burstein, ETS (USA)
Rickard Domeij, The Language Council of Sweden (Sweden)
Kevin Egan, University of Southern California (USA)
Caroline Hagège, Xerox Research Centre Europe (France)
Soe Johansson Kokkinakis, University of Gothenburg (Sweden)
Ola Karlsson, The Language Council of Sweden (Sweden)
Ola Knutsson, KTH (Sweden)
Sabine Lehmann, acrolinx GmbH (Switzerland)
Eva Lindgren, Umeå University (Sweden)
Aurlien Max, LIMSI (France)
Guido Nottbusch, University of Bielefeld (Germany)
Daniel Perrin, Zurich University of Applied Sciences (Switzerland)
Martin Reynaert, Tilburg University (The Netherlands)
Gert Rijlaarsdam, University of Amsterdam (The Netherlands)
Dietmar Rösner, Otto-von-Guericke University Magdeburg (Germany)
Koenraad de Smedt, University of Bergen (Norway)
Sylvana Sofkova Hashemi, University of Gothenburg (Sweden)
Scott Warnock, Drexel University (USA)
Eric Wehrli, University of Geneva (Switzerland)
Carl Whithaus, UC Davis (USA)
Michael Zock, CNRS (France)

Table of Contents

Workshop Program

Sunday, June 6, 2010

09:00 Opening

Session 1

09:15–09:40 *Computational Linguistics in the Translator's Workflow—Combining Authoring Tools and Translation Memory Systems*
Christoph Rösener

09:40–10:05 *Scientific Authoring Support: A Tool to Navigate in Typed Citation Graphs*
Ulrich Schäfer and Uwe Kasterka

10:05–10:30 *Grammaticality Judgement in a Word Completion Task*
Alfred Renaud, Fraser Shein and Vivian Tsang

10:30 Coffee Break

Session 2

11:00–11:25 *The Design of a Proofreading Software Service*
Raphael Mudge

11:25–11:50 *A Toolkit to Assist L2 Learners Become Independent Writers*
John Milton and Vivying S.Y. Cheng

11:50–12:15 *Learning Simple Wikipedia: A Cogitation in Ascertaining Abecedarian Language*
Courtney Napoles and Mark Dredze

12:15 Lunch Break

Sunday, June 6, 2010 (continued)

Session 3

1:40–2:05	*Questions Worth Asking: Intersections between Writing Research and Computational Linguistics* Anne Ruggles Gere and Laura Aull
2:05–2:30	*Exploring Individual Differences in Student Writing with a Narrative Composition Support Environment* Julius Goth, Alok Baikadi, Eun Young Ha, Jonathan Rowe, Bradford Mott and James Lester
2:30–2:55	*The Linguistics of Readability: The Next Step for Word Processing* Neil Newbold and Lee Gillam
3:00	Coffee Break

Discussion

3:30	Discussion
5:00	Closing

Computational Linguistics in the Translator's Workflow—Combining Authoring Tools and Translation Memory Systems

Christoph Rösener
Institute of Applied Information Sciences (IAI)
Martin-Luther-Straße 14
D-66111 Saarbrücken, Germany
chrisr@iai-sb.de

Abstract

In Technical Documentation, Authoring Tools are used to maintain a consistent text quality—especially with regard to the often followed translation of the original documents into several languages using a Translation Memory System. Hitherto these tools have often been used separately one after the other. Additionally Authoring tools often have no linguistic intelligence and thus the quality level of the automated checks is very poor. In this paper I will describe the integration of a linguistically intelligent Authoring Tool into a Translation Memory System, thereby combining linguistic intelligence with the advantages of both systems in a single environment. The system allows you not only the use of common authoring aids (spell, grammar and style checker) in source and target language—by using a single environment the terminology database of the Translation Memory System can be used by the authoring aid to control terminology both in the source and target document. Moreover, the linguistically intelligent Authoring Tool enables automatic extraction of term candidates from existing documents directly to the terminology database of the Translation Memory System.

1 Introduction

The benefit of Authoring Tools, especially in the area of Technical Documentation, is beyond debate (cf. Brockmann, 1997, Huijsen, 1998, Nyberg et al., 2003, Spyridakis et al., 1997). Combined with linguistic intelligence besides spell and grammar checking Authoring Tools are used to check terminology, style, and abbreviations in texts (cf. Bredenkamp et al., 2000, Carl et al., 2002b, Haller 2000, Reuther and Wigger, 2000). In most cases this is done in relation to special style guides and terminology, both given by the respective company (cf. O'Brien, 2003, Reuther, 2003, Shubert et al., 1995). Due to the fact that Authoring Aids are mostly used as a single application, style rules and terminology are kept and maintained in a special database together with the application. Moreover linguistically intelligent Authoring Aids also help the author to extract terminology candidates. Subsequently, where required, these candidates can be directly imported into the stored terminology. To enable this function it is also necessary to have the terminology database integrated in the application.

When translating technical documents it has for many years been common practice to use Translation Memory Systems to improve the consistency of translations. Translation Memory Systems store whole sentences or clauses (segments) and their translations in a multi-language translation memory. When the translator is translating a new document the segments are matched against those already present in the translation memory. This is done with the help of a fuzzy match algorithm, which calculates the degree of similarity between the current source segment and matching source segments from the translation memory. The degree of similarity is expressed as a percentage value (100% match means identical match). The matches are afterwards presented in descending order and the translator can paste them into the new translation.

Proceedings of the NAACL HLT 2010 Workshop on Computational Linguistics and Writing, pages 1–6,
Los Angeles, California, June 2010.

Besides the translation memory most of the Translation Memory Systems also have an integrated terminology database. On the basis of this database the system is able to suggest translations of single terms even when there is no match on sentence or clause level. The matching of terms is also done with fuzzy matching algorithms. Therefore related as well as identical terms are found in the database. With this function the Translation Memory System offers to some extent a feature similar to the Authoring Tools mentioned above. Yet the quality of the feature implemented in Translation Memory Systems is not the same due to the fact that in most cases this feature in Translation Memory Systems works without linguistic intelligence.

When using both tools, the Authoring Tool as well as the Translation Memory System as a single application, the main problem becomes immediately apparent: the double terminology database. Two terminology databases—Authoring Tool and Translation Memory System—, which have to be maintained in different applications, mean a lot of redundant work.

The other possibility—regular synchronizing of the databases—is very difficult, because it is not clear, which of the databases is the core database. Generally speaking, the author manually enters new terms in the context of translations into the terminology database of the Translation Memory System, whereas the results of automatic term extractions are stored in the terminology database of the Authoring Tool.

In the following I will present a system where the Authoring Tool is directly integrated in the Translation Memory workflow, thus allowing the handling of terminology in only one core database. It is the integration of CLAT (Controlled Language Authoring Tool) into the Across Translation Memory System—the crossAuthor Linguistic.

2 Description

For the understanding of the system and how the particular components work together it is necessary to begin with a description of the underlying modules. The system consists mainly of three modules: the CLAT/UMMT software package, the Across Language Server and the crossAuthor / crossAuthor Linguistic add-on.

2.1 CLAT/UMMT

CLAT/UMMT is a software package from the IAI (Institut der Gesellschaft zur Förderung der Angewandten Informationsforschung an der Universität des Saarlandes—Institute of the Society for the Promotion of Applied Information Sciences at Saarland University). CLAT is a tool designed to support technical authors in producing high-quality documentation (e.g., according to specific standards (cf. DIN ISO 12620, 1999, Herzog and Mühlbauer, 2007)). This is reached through linguistic correctness and compliance with company-specific requirements. CLAT offers

- spell and grammar checking to verify linguistic correctness
- style and terminology checking to verify compliance with company-specific writing guidelines

The CLAT spelling checker elicits incorrectly spelt or unknown words (e.g., *proplusion*). Besides that the CLAT spelling checker can also be used to check British versus American English (e.g., *organise* vs. *organize*). The CLAT grammar checker elicits grammatically incorrect sentences or parts of sentences (e.g., *He come*). In addition, typography errors that involve more than one word or character are also detected.

Stylistic weaknesses in terms of clarity, understandability, and stylistic appropriateness of sentences or parts of sentences are corrected by the CLAT style checker. Especially complexity issues (e.g., too many uses of *and* and *or*), ambiguity issues (e.g., indefinite or anaphoric expressions, such as *it, they, these,* those), as well as stylistic problems (e.g., contracted forms such as *they've*) are detected. Typically this is done on the basis of company-specific writing rules. Finally, the CLAT terminology checker elicits variants of preferred terms, as well as deprecated terms and admitted terms. When the terminology checker finds a deprecated term in the text, a message is displayed with the corresponding preferred term (e.g., *electric engine*—deprecated term, *electric motor*—preferred term) for correction.

In addition to the four standard checking functions CLAT also offers a function for eliciting term candidates. This function is not a checking function in the sense that it finds linguistic errors or weaknesses. Rather, it supports the terminology workflow of a company. Nouns that have the properties typical of terms and have not been found during the check in the database, either as correctly used terms or variants or deprecated terms, are listed in a separate display window together with the context they occurred in. The author then has the possibility to decide whether any of the term candidates should be included in the terminology of the respective company.

CLAT checks documents with regard to the control functions mentioned above, reports every rule violation and gives technical authors the opportunity to revise their text and immediately re-check the corrections made. CLAT offers an additional function for working in editors that support tags (e.g., FrameMaker). This function, a context-sensitive search, enables the individual processing of individual tags. With the help of a DTD that must be created especially for CLAT, the CLAT server can process tags differently and ignore their contents entirely or only for individual style rules.

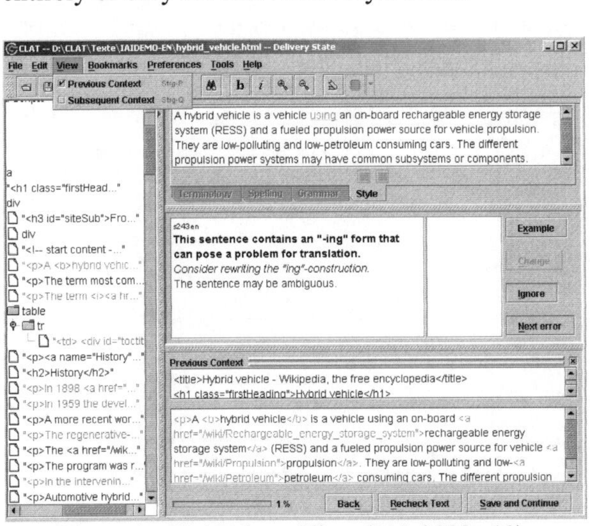

Figure 1. CLAT-Java Client (IAI, 2009a:10).

All CLAT checks are based on a linguistic analysis of the text document. The linguistic analysis consists of several steps that are described in the following:

- separating linguistic from non-linguistic data
- recognizing word boundaries
- analysing word forms: morphological analysis
- determining part of speech: grammatical analysis

The CLAT system consists of a CLAT server and CLAT Clients. CLAT Clients are user interfaces that are either stand-alone (Java CLAT Client) or they are CLAT-Ins that are plugged into an existing word processing program. The CLAT server handles the communication between the CLAT Clients and the Linguistic Engine. The Linguistic Engine is the core part of the CLAT system. It performs the linguistic analysis and the CLAT checks.

The main component of the Linguistic Engine is the program MPRO for the morphological and syntactic analysis of the given text. For further details on MPRO see Maas et al. (2009).

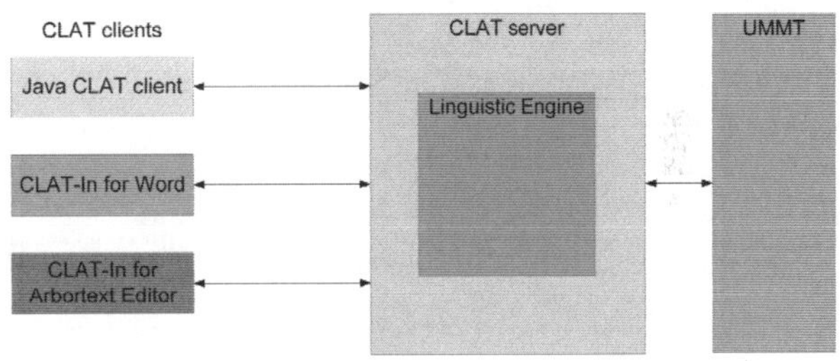

Figure 2. Architecture of the CLAT System (IAI, 2009b:4)

Due to the Linguistic Engine the quality level of the CLAT checks is very high, e.g. the morphological analysis enables CLAT to elicit morphological word form variants such as *electrical battery* as a variant of *electric battery*. Moreover due to the linguistic intelligence CLAT is able to detect even word order variants such as *source of propulsion power* as a variant of *propulsion power source*. These variants are found using complex methods of linguistic abstraction and do not need to be explicitly named in the terminological database (cf. Carl et al., 2002a, Hong et al., 2001, Thurmair, 2003).

Another system component of CLAT is UMMT (Utility for Mandate Management Tasks). It is the central configuration tool for the CLAT-Server. With UMMT, language resources used in CLAT are created, updated, and administered according to the requirements of the respective company.

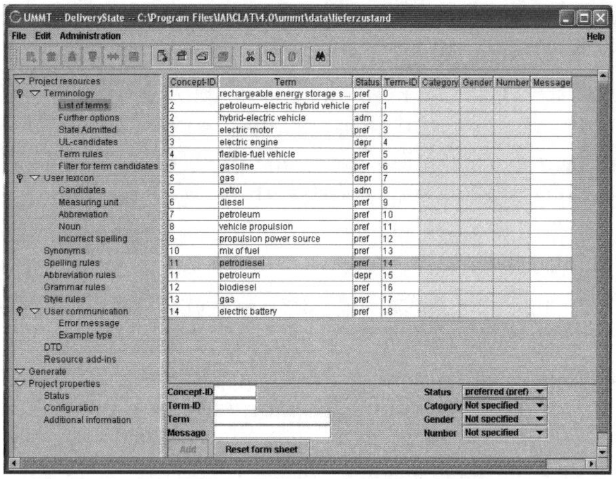

Figure 3. UMMT configuration tool for the CLAT-Server (IAI, 2010:19).

Some of the possible settings for CLAT projects in UMMT are:

- import/maintenance of terminology
- definition of stylistic and grammatical rules
- definition of special spellings and synonyms

All these settings are saved as a project and can be accessed by CLAT at run time. The central project and user management of UMMT allows creation and administration of CLAT projects as well as CLAT users or user groups. CLAT projects can be assigned to one or several CLAT users or user groups. For more detailed information about the CLAT/UMMT Software package see the IAI User Manuals (IAI, 2009a/b).

2.2 Across Language Server

The Across Language Server is the central software platform of the Across language system. The software includes a translation memory, a terminology system, and project management and translation workflow control tools. In this paper I will describe only a few components of the software—the translation memory, the terminology database and the user interface. For further information on the Across Language Server see the Across User Manuals (Across, 2009b/c).

The translation memory within the Across language server—called crossTank—contains sentence pairs from earlier translations. If it finds an identical or similar sentence in a new source text, it offers the stored translation as the basis for an optional automatic pre-translation or as a suggestion, as soon as the translator has arrived at the relevant sentence of the source text in the editor. New translations can either be saved automatically in crossTank or the translator can also choose to save them manually.

The terminology database within the Across Language Server—called crossTerm—enables the translator to create and update multilingual sets of terminology, in particular company-specific terminology and glossaries of technical terms. crossTerm stores concepts and their verbal designations (e. g., translation, synonym, antonym, etc.) for all languages at a single level. It is possible to store many different types of additional information, as well as user-defined information.
Both modules—the translation memory and the database—are integrated in a central user interface—called crossDesk. It provides the translator with a text editor for the source and the target text as well as the functions mentioned above. Matches in crossTank and crossTerm are marked in the source text automatically and can be easily incorporated into the target text.

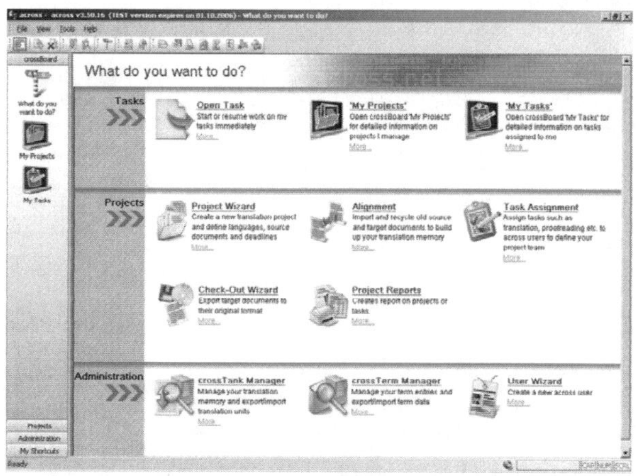

Figure 4. Central user interface crossDesk (Across, 2009d:24).

2.3 crossAuthor / crossAuthor Linguistic

crossAuthor and crossAuthor Linguistic are add-ons for separate source-text editors (e.g., MS Word, Adobe FrameMaker) and provide an interface to the Across Language Server. With crossAuthor, the sentence the user is currently working on in the source-text editor is sent to the Across Language Server. This sentence will then be searched for in crossTank. Relevant search hits are sent back to the user and are displayed in the corresponding crossTank window. At the same time crossTerm is searched for any corresponding words in the current sentence. The relevant search hits are also transmitted to the crossAuthor add-on via the interface and displayed in the crossTerm window.

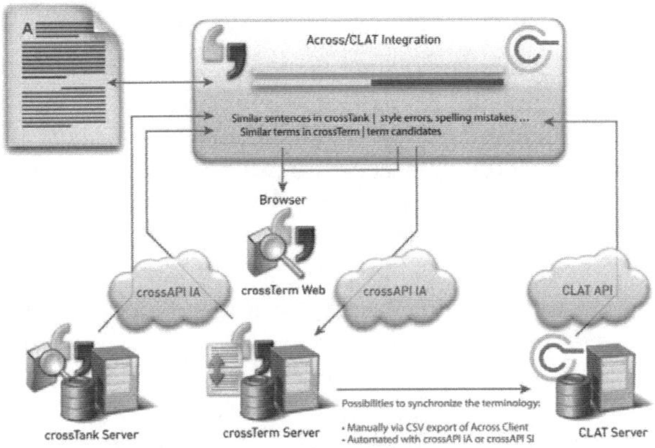

Figure 5. Across/CLAT Integration (Across, 2009a:40).

Finally, crossAuthor Linguistic is an expanded solution of crossAuthor featuring seamless integration of CLAT in Across. With crossAuthor Linguistic users have access to the crossTank and crossTerm matches as well as to the CLAT results.

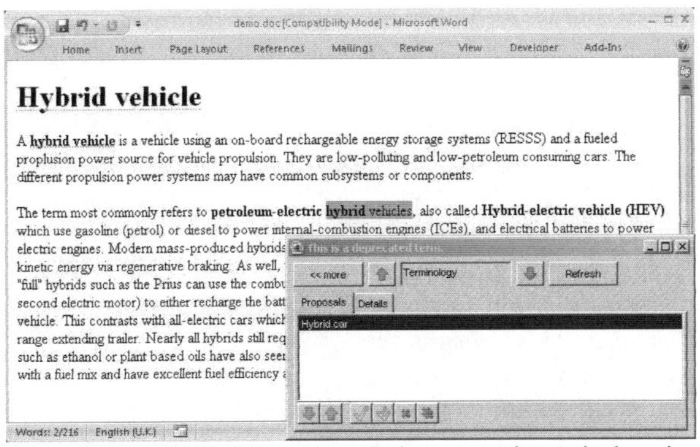

Figure 6. crossAuthor Linguistic correction window in MS Word 2003 (Across, 2009a:48).

Moreover, the CLAT connection enables the direct integration of the editor in the terminology creation process. With the CLAT term-candidate extraction, the editor can directly save auto-detected and extracted terminology as entries in the crossTerm database. As a result, crossTerm works as a core terminology database for both systems. To make the CLAT server work with the respective terminology it is only necessary to import the terminology into UMMT before starting CLAT. This can be done either manually via CSV or automatically by a special interface.

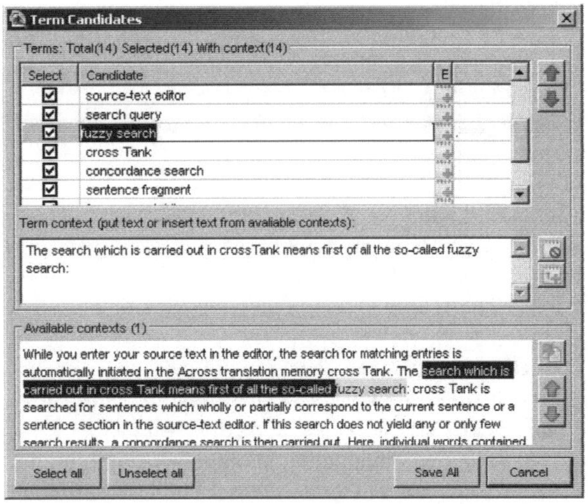

Figure 7. Term-candidate extraction in crossAuthor (Across, 2009a:50).

3 Conclusion

The integration of Authoring tools into Translation Memory Systems is an important step towards a single working environment for the translator's workflow. The system described enables the translator to maintain the terminology for both systems—the Authoring Tool as well as the Translation Memory System—in a single core database. Moreover, the integration of CLAT in Across allows the translator to save auto-detected and extracted term-candidates directly into this database.

Due to the linguistically intelligent analysis in CLAT it is necessary to have specific information about the terms (part of speech, gender, etc.). This information is automatically generated within the CLAT System. This is the reason why the described system actually still has two separate terminology databases. But this is not an important disadvantage of the overall system as long as one of the databases is the core database. The fact, that only one core database has to be maintained means a significant reduction of the workload of translators resp. terminologists.

The system presented is only a first step towards a fully integrated solution for the translators working environment. The focus for future research could be for example the development of an integrated linguistic intelligent Authoring Tool to proof whole translation memories.

References

Across Systems GmbH. 2009a. *User Manual. Translation-Oriented Authoring with crossAuthor / crossAuthor Linguistic v. 5.0.*

Across Systems GmbH. 2009b. *Across Step by Step. Unser Manual v. 5.0.*

Across Systems GmbH. 2009c. *Across at a glance. User Manual v. 5.0.*

Across Systems GmbH. 2009d. *Quickstart Across Language Server v. 5.0.*

Andrew Bredenkamp, Berthold Crysman, and Mirela Petrea. 2000. Building Multilingual Controlled Language Performance Checkers. In Adriaens et al. (Eds), *Proceedings of the Third International Workshop on Controlled Language Applications (CLAW 2000),* Seattle, Washington, pp. 83–89.

Daniel Brockmann. 1997. Controlled Language & Translation Memory Technology: a Perfect Match to Save Translation Cost. *TC Forum 4/97,* pp. 10–11.

Michael Carl, Johann Haller, Christoph Horschmann, and Axel Theofilidis. 2002a. A Hybrid Example-Based Approach for Detecting Terminological Variants in Documents and Lists of Terms. *6. Konferenz zur Verarbeitung natürlicher Sprache, KONVENS,* Saarbrücken. http://www.iai-sb.de/docs/konvens.pdf.

Michael Carl, Johann Haller, Christoph Horschmann, Dieter Maas, and Jörg Schütz. 2002b. *The TETRIS Terminology Tool.* In *TAL*, Vol. 43:1. http://www.iai-sb.de/docs/ tal.pdf.

DIN ISO 12620. 1999. *Computer Applications in Terminology – Data Categories.*

Gottfried Herzog and Holger Mühlbauer. 2007. *Normen für Übersetzer und technische Autoren.* Beuth Verlag GmbH, Berlin.

Johann Haller. 2000. MULTIDOC – Authoring Aids for Multilingual Technical Documentation. *First Congress of Specialized Translation*, Barcelona, March 2000. http://www.iai-sb.de/docs/bcn.pdf.

Willem-Olaf Huijsen. 1998. Controlled Language – An Introduction. In Mitamura et al. (Eds), *Proceedings of the Second International Workshop on Controlled Language Applications – CLAW 98,* Language Technologies Institute, Carnegie Mellon University, Pittsburgh, Pennsylvania, pp. 1–15.

Munpyo Hong , Sisay Fissaha, and Johann Haller. 2001. Hybrid filtering for extraction of term candidates from German technical texts. *TIA-2001*, Nancy. http://www.iai-sb.de/docs/term_extract.pdf.

IAI (Institut der Gesellschaft zur Förderung der Angwandten Informationsforschung). 2009a. *CLAT-Client Manual 4.1*

IAI (Institut der Gesellschaft zur Förderung der Angwandten Informationsforschung). 2009b. *CLAT-Introduction Version 4.1*

IAI (Institut der Gesellschaft zur Förderung der Angwandten Informationsforschung). 2010. *UMMT Manual Version 4.1*

Heinz-Dieter Maas, Christoph Rösener, and Axel Theofilidis. 2009. Morphosyntactic and Semantic Analysis of Text: The MPRO Tagging Procedure. In: Cerstin Mahlow and Michael Piotrowski (Eds.): *State of the art in computational morphology. Workshop on systems and frameworks for computational morphology, SFCM 2009, Zurich, Switzerland, September 4, 2009.* Proceedings. New York: Springer (Communications in Computer and Information Science, 41), pp. 76–87.

Eric Nyberg, Teruko Mitamura, and Willem-Olaf Huijsen. 2003. Controlled Language for Authoring and Translation. In H. Somers. (ed), *Computers ad Translation: A Translator's Guide,* Amsterdam, John Benjamins, pp. 245–282.

Sharon O'Brien. 2003. Controlling Controlled English – An Analysis of Several Controlled Language Rule Sets. *Proceedings of the Joint Conference combining the 8th International Workshop of the European Association for Machine Translation and the 4th Controlled Language Applications Workshop (CLAW 2003),* 15th–17th May, Dublin City University, Dublin, Ireland, pp. 105–114.

Ursula Reuther. 2003. Two in One – Can it Work? Readability and Translatability by means of Controlled Language. *Proceedings of the Joint Conference combining the 8th International Workshop of the European Association for Machine Translation and the 4th Controlled Language Applications Workshop (CLAW 2003),* 15th–17th May, Dublin City University, Dublin, Ireland, pp. 124–132.

Ursula Reuther and Antje Schmidt-Wigger. 2000. Designing a Multi-Purpose CL Application. In Adriaens et al. (eds), *Proceedings of the Third International Workshop on Controlled Language Applications (CLAW 2000),* Seattle, Washington, pp. 72–82.

Serena Shubert, Jan Spyridakis, and Heather Holmback. 1995. The Comprehensibility of Simplified English in Procedures. *Journal of Technical Writing and Communication,* 25(4):347–369.

Jan Spyridakis, Serena Shubert, and Heather Holmback. 1997. Measuring the Translatability of Simplified English in Procedural Documents. *IEEE Transactions on Professional Communication.* 40(1):217–246.

Gregor Thurmair. 2003. Making Term Extraction Tools Usable. *Proceedings of the Joint Conference combining the 8th International Workshop of the European Association for Machine Translation and the 4th Controlled Language Applications Workshop (CLAW 2003),* 15th–17th May, Dublin City University, Dublin, Ireland, pp. 170–179.

Scientific Authoring Support: A Tool to Navigate in Typed Citation Graphs

Ulrich Schäfer
Language Technology Lab
German Research Center for
Artificial Intelligence (DFKI)
D-66123 Saarbrücken, Germany
ulrich.schaefer@dfki.de

Uwe Kasterka
Computer Science Department
Saarland University
Campus
D-66123 Saarbrücken, Germany
uwe.kasterka@dfki.de

Abstract

Scientific authors urgently need help in managing the fast increasing number of publications. We describe and demonstrate a tool that supports authors in browsing graphically through electronically available publications, thus allowing them to quickly adapt to new domains and publish faster. Navigation is assisted by means of typed citation graphs, i.e. we use methods and resources from computational linguistics to compute the kind of citation that is made from one paper to another (refutation, use, confirmation etc.). To verify the computed citation type, the user can inspect the highlighted citation sentence in the original PDF document. While our classification methods used to generate a realistic test data set are relatively simple and could be combined with other proposed approaches, we put a strong focus on usability and quick navigation in the potentially huge graphs. In the outlook, we argue that our tool could be made part of a community approach to overcome the sparseness and correctness dilemma in citation classification.

1 Introduction and Motivation

According to different studies, the number of scientific works is doubled every 5-10 years. Important issues to be addressed by the scientific community are finding relevant information and avoiding redundancy and duplication of work. The organization and preservation of scientific knowledge in scientific publications, vulgo text documents, thwarts these efforts. From a viewpoint of a computer scientist, scientific papers are just 'unstructured information'.

One specific, but very important aspect of the content of scientific papers is their relation to previous work and, once published, their impact to subsequent or derived research. While it is still hard if not impossible to capture and formalize the semantic content of a scientific publication automatically, at least citation properties and derived scientific impact can be and usually are measured automatically on the basis of simple citation graphs. In other words, these graphs can be used to describe I/O behavior of publications in a very simple way.

However, just counting citations is a very coarse approach and does not tell much about the reasons for citing one's work in a specific situation. Moreover, once such measure is formalized and standardized e.g. for science evaluation, it can be exploited to tune up statistics. Since the first proposal of the Science Citation Index (Garfield, 1955), it has also provoked criticism.

In the bibliometrics and computational linguistics literature, many proposals are available on how citations could be further classified by careful analysis of citation sentences and context (Garfield, 1965; Garzone, 1996; Mercer and Di Marco, 2004; Teufel et al., 2006; Bornmann and Daniel, 2008).

The number of different classes proposed varies from 3 to 35. Different authors try to identify dimensions and mutually exclusive classes, but the more classes a schema contains, the more difficult becomes the automatic classification.

The focus of our paper is to combine automatic classification approaches with a tool that supports scientists in graphically navigating through *typed citation graphs (TCG)*. Such TCGs can be generated

Proceedings of the NAACL HLT 2010 Workshop on Computational Linguistics and Writing, pages 7–14,
Los Angeles, California, June 2010.

by augmenting a simple citation graph with information synonymously called citation *function* (Teufel et al., 2006), citation *relation* (Mercer and Di Marco, 2004) or citation *sentiment*, forming the labels of the graph's edges. In the following, we use the more neutral and general term *citation type*.

The idea is to help scientists, especially those not so familiar with an area, understanding the relations between publications and quickly get an overview of the field. Moreover, the goal is to embed this tool in a larger framework for scientists that also supports semantic search assisted by domain ontologies and further tools for authoring support (Schäfer et al., 2008).

Our paper is structured as follows. In Section 2, we describe how we automatically compute the typed citation graph from the raw text content of a scientific paper corpus to generate realistic data for testing the visualization and navigation tool. Section 3 contains an evaluation of the quality of the extracted unlabeled graphs and of the citation classification step. We then describe in Section 4 the ideas of efficient and at the same time well-arranged visualization and navigation in the typed citation graph. We compare with related work in Section 5. Finally, we conclude and give an outlook to future work in Section 6.

2 Data Preparation and Automatic Citation Type Classification

Our corpus is based on 6300 electronically-available papers, a subset (published 2002-2008) of the ACL Anthology (Bird et al., 2008), a comprehensive collection of scientific conference and workshop papers in the area of computational linguistics and language technology.

The overall workflow of the employed tools and data is shown in Fig. 1.

We ran the open source tool ParsCit (Councill et al., 2008) to extract references lists and corresponding citation sentences from raw paper texts. To build the citation graph, we used the Levenshtein distance (Levenshtein, 1966) to find and match titles and authors of identical papers yet tolerating spelling and PDF extraction errors.

To increase robustness, publication years were not considered as they would hinder matches for

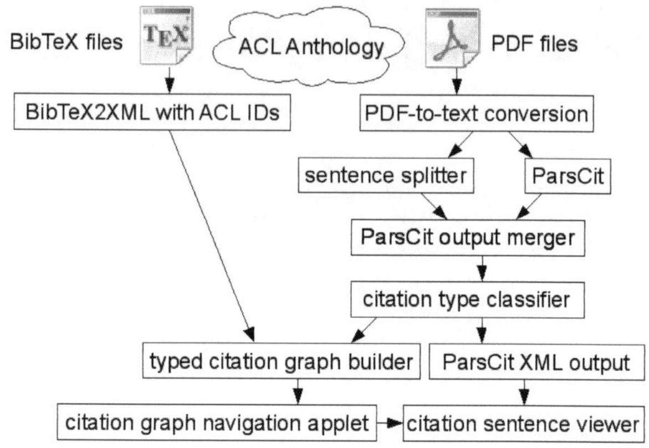

Figure 1: Workflow from ACL Anthology data (top) to citation graph navigation applet and citation sentence viewer (bottom)

delayed journal publications. Generation of the graph edges, i.e. matching of papers and reference strings, is performed by means of the ACL ID, a unique identifier for each paper, available for the PDF (source nodes of references) and BibTeX files (targets of references).

We evaluated the generated graph against the one that was corrected manually by the ACL Anthology Network (AAN) group (Radev et al., 2009) and found that 10821 citation links were shared between both and can be considered correct[1].

3883 additional ones were in the AAN but not recognized by us, the other way round, 1021 discovered by us were not in the AAN. In addition, the publication bases were not identical. The anthology network data ends in February 2007 but covers years before 2002, while our data covers 2002-2008 inclusively. Given the fact that our graph is computed fully automatically, the result can be considered very good.

In the next step, we augmented the citation graph by types for each edge. In contrast to other approaches, we currently only consider the citation sentence itself to determine the citation type, neither a wider context, its position nor the abstract, title or content of the cited paper. A reference (from the references section at the end of a paper) may be associated with several citation sentences mentioning the paper referenced at the end.

[1]We only consider intra-network links here, not those pointing to books or other publications outside the corpus.

In only considering the citation sentence itself, we may lose some citation type information, as it may be (also) contained in follow-up sentences referring to the citation using a pronoun ("they", "their approach" etc.). Considering follow-up or even preceding sentences is planned to be addressed in future work.

After consulting the rich literature on citation classification (Bornmann and Daniel, 2008; Garzone, 1996; Teufel et al., 2006), we derived a simplified classification schema consisting of the following five classes.

- Agree: The citing paper agrees with the cited paper
- PRecycle: The citing paper uses an algorithm, data, method or tool from the cited paper
- Negative: The paper is cited negatively/contrastively
- Neutral: The paper is cited neutrally
- Undef: impossible determine the sentiment of the citation (fallback)

Then, we used a blend of methods to collect verbal and non-verbal patterns (cue words) and associated each with a class from the aforementioned schema.

- A list from (Garzone, 1996) devised for biomedical texts; it is largely applicable to the computational linguistics domain as well.
- Simple negation of positive cue words to obtain negative patterns.
- A list of automatically extracted synonyms and antonyms (the latter for increasing number of patterns for negative citations) from WordNet (Miller et al., 1993).
- Automatically computed most frequent cooccurrences from all extracted citation sentences of the corpus using an open source cooccurrence tool (Banerjee and Pedersen, 2003).
- Inspection: browse and filter cue words manually, remove redundancies.

3 Results: Distribution and Evaluation

These pattern where then used for the classification algorithm and applied to the extracted citation sentences. In case of multiple citations with different classes, a voting mechanism was applied were the 'stronger' classes (Agree, Negative, PRecycle) won in standoff cases. For the total of 91419 citations we obtained the results shown in Table 1.

Classes	Citations	Percent
Agree	3513	3.8%
Agree, Neutral	2020	2.2%
Negative	1147	1.2%
PRecycle	10609	11.6%
PRecycle, Agree	1419	1.6%
PRecycle, Agree, Neutral	922	1.0%
PRecycle, Neutral	3882	4.2%
Neutral	13430	14.7%
Undef	54837	60.0%

Table 1: Citation classification result

The numbers reflect a careful classification approach where uncertain citations are classified as Undef. In case of multiple matches, the first (leftmost) was taken to achieve a unique result.

The results also confirm obervations made in other works: (1) citation classification is a hard task, (2) there are only a few strongly negative citations which coincides with observations made by (Teufel et al., 2006), (Pendlebury, 2009) and others, (3) the majority of citations is neutral or of unknown type.

An evaluation on a test set of 100 citations spread across all the types of papers with a manual check of the accuracy of the computed labels showed an overall accuracy of 30% mainly caused by the fact that 90% of undefined hits were in fact neutral (i.e., labeling all undefs neutral would increase accuracy). Negative citations are sparse and unreliable (33%), neutral ones are about 60% accurate, PRecycle: 33%, Agree: 25%.

To sum up, our automatic classification approach based on only local citation information could surely be improved by applying methods described in the literature, but it helped us to quickly (without annotation effort) generate a plausible data set for the main task, visualization and navigation in the typed citation graphs.

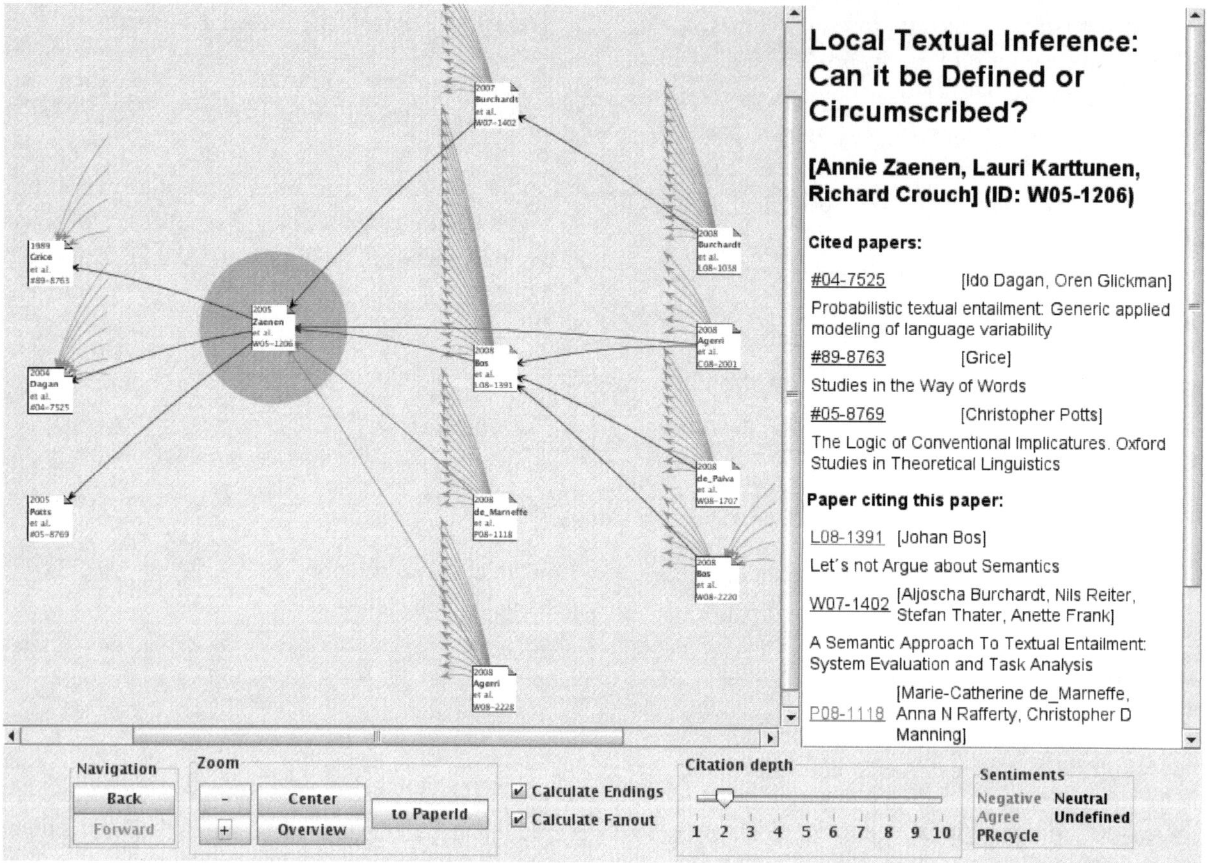

Figure 2: Typed citation graph navigator applet

4 Visualization Algorithm and Navigation User Interface

The overall idea of the citation visualization and navigation tool is simple and intuitive. Each paper is represented by a node, all citations between papers are drawn as edges between nodes where the color of the edge indicates the computed (overall) citation type, e.g. green for agree, red for negative, blue for recycle and black for neutral or undefined.

To cope with flexible layouts and scalability of the graph, we decided to use the open source tool Java Universal Network/Graph Framework (JUNG, http://jung.sourceforge.net). Its main advantages over similar tools are that it supports user interaction (clicking on nodes and edges, tool tips) and user-implemented graph layout algorithms. A screenshot of the final user interface is presented in Figure 2.

The decision for and development of the visualization and navigation tool was mainly driven by the fact that citation graphs quickly grow and become unmanagable by humans when extended to the transitive closures of citing or cited papers of a given publication. The sheer number of crossing edges would make the display unreadable.

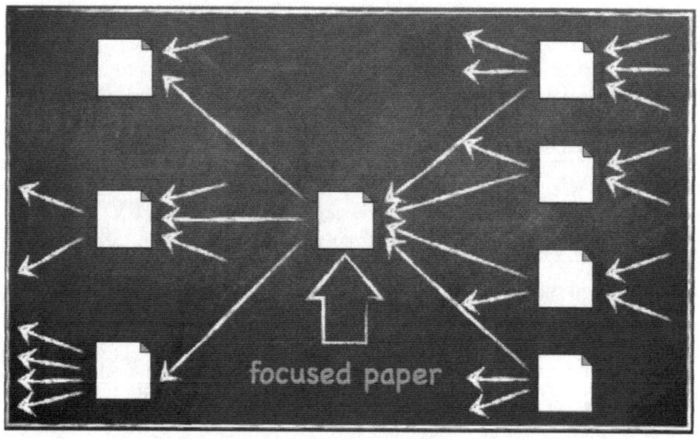

Figure 3: Focused paper in the center

The main design goal therefore was reducing the number of nodes and edges where possible and (by default) have only one paper in focus (Fig. 3), with all cited papers on the left side (Fig. 4), and all citing papers on the right (Fig. 5).

This also reflects a time line order where the origin (oldest papers) is on the left. In the graphical user interface, the citation depth (default 1) is adjustable by a slider to higher numbers. The graph display is updated upon change of the configured depth.

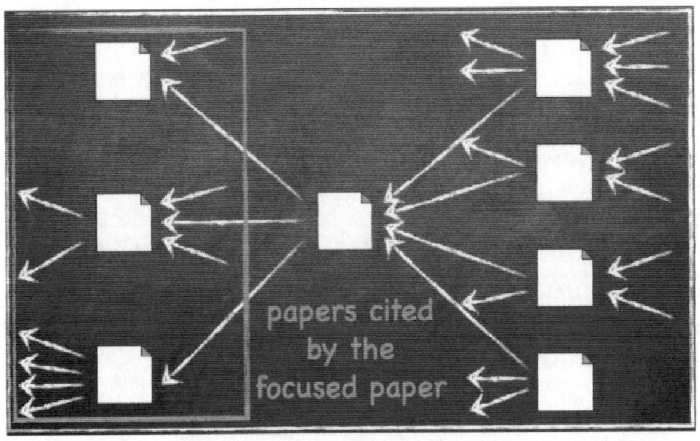

Figure 4: Papers cited by the focused paper

At level 1, papers citing the citing papers (analogously for cited papers), are not fully drawn as nodes, but only adumbrated by short ingoing or outgoing edges (arrows). However, the color of these short edges still signifies the citation type and may attract interest which can easily be satisfied by clicking on the edge's remaining node (cf. screenshot in Figure 2). When the mouse is moved over a node, a tooltip text display pops up displaying full author list and paper title.

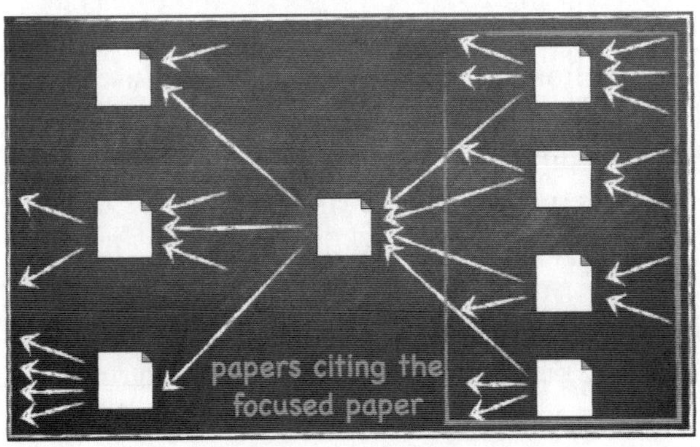

Figure 5: Papers citing the focused paper

To avoid crossing edges caused by citations at the same level (citing or cited papers also cite each other), we devised a fan-out layout generation (Fig. 6). It increases the width of the displayed graph, but leads to better readability. Fan-out layout can also be switched off in the user interface.

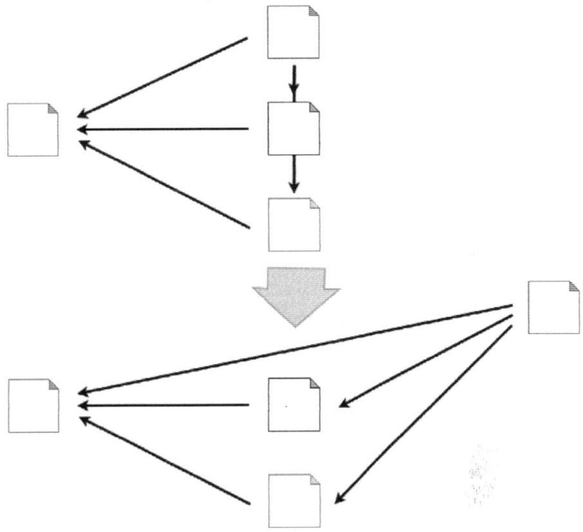

Figure 6: Fan-out layout: avoid crossing edges caused by citations on the same level

In addition, the graph layout algorithm orders papers chronologically in the vertical direction. Here, we have implemented another technique that helps to avoid crossing edges. As shown in Fig. 7, we sort papers vertically by also taking into account the position of its predecessor, the cited paper. It often leads to less crossing edges.

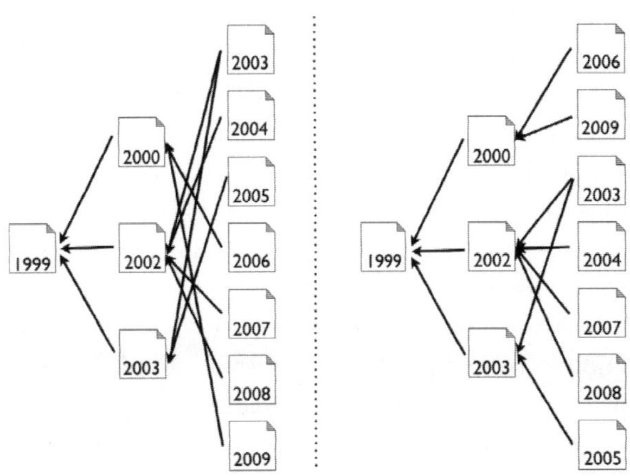

Figure 7: Order: avoid crossing edges by ordering chronologically (strict, simple variant on the left for comparison), taking into account the position of the cited paper on the previous level (right)

By double-clicking on any node representing a paper (cited or citing), this node can be made the new center and the graph is re-arranged accordingly.

Zooming in and out is possible via mouse wheel or shortcut buttons ('overview', 'center').

Using the right mouse button context menu on a node, it is possible to open a details page for the selected paper with bibliographic metadata and all citations and types. All references in the document with their citation sentences identified are displayed in a structured list.

The citation context around a citation sentence is shown as well, while the citation sentence itself is colored according to the citation type color and clickable. If clicked, the original PDF document opens with the citation sentence highlighted (Fig. 8; currently only possible in Acrobat Reader).

By clicking on an edge instead of a node, only the citations between the two papers at both ends are displayed, in the same way as described above for all citations of a document.

5 Related Work

Our paper touches and combines results of three disciplines, (1) bibliometrics, (2) computational linguistics, and (3) information visualization. We briefly discuss related and mostly recent literature, being aware of the fact that this list is necessarily incomplete.

(Garfield, 1965) is probably the first to discuss an automatic computation of citation types. He is also the founder of citation indexing and the Institute of Scientific Information (ISI). His first publication on science citation indexing appeared in 1955 (Garfield, 1955) and he remained the probably most influential scientist in this field for decades. (Bornmann and Daniel, 2008) is a comprehensive recent metastudy on citing behavior.

Investigating citation classification has a long tradition in bibliometrics and information science and in the last 20 years also attracted computational linguistics researchers trying to automate the task based on rhetorics of science, statistical methods and sentence parsing.

There is much more work than we can cite here on citation function computation worth combination with our approach (Bornmann and Daniel, 2008; Garzone, 1996; Teufel et al., 2006) – using our tool one can easily browse to further publications!

There is little work on innovative layout techniques for displaying and navigating citation graphs. We found three independent approaches to citation graph visualization: CiteViz (Elmqvist and Tsigas, 2004), CircleView (Bergström and Jr., 2006), and (Nguyen et al., 2007). They share a disadvantageous property in that they try to visualize too much information at the same time. In our opinion, this contradicts the need to navigate and keep control over displayable parts of large paper collections.

Moreover, these approaches do not provide information on citation types derived from text as our system does. Further ideas on visualizing science-related information such as author co-citation networks are also discussed and summarized in (Chen, 2006).

6 Summary and Outlook

We have presented an innovative tool to support scientific authors in browsing graphically through large collections of publications by means of typed citation graphs. To quickly generate a realistic data set, we devised a classification approach avoiding manual annotation and intervention.

Our classification results cannot compete with approaches such as (Teufel et al., 2006) based on considerable manual annotation for machine learning. However, we think that our application could be combined with this or other approaches described for classifying citations between scientific papers.

We envisage to integrate the navigation tool in a larger framework supporting scientific authoring (Schäfer et al., 2008). When publishing a service of this kind on the Web, one would be faced with ethical issues such as the problem that authors could feel offended by wrongly classified citations.

The reason is that citation type classification is potentially even more subjective than a bare citation index—which itself is already highly controversal, as discussed in the introduction. Moreover, there is not always a single, unique citation type, but often vagueness and room for interpretation.

Therefore, we suggest to augment such a service by a Web 2.0 application that would allow registered users to confirm, alter and annotate precom-

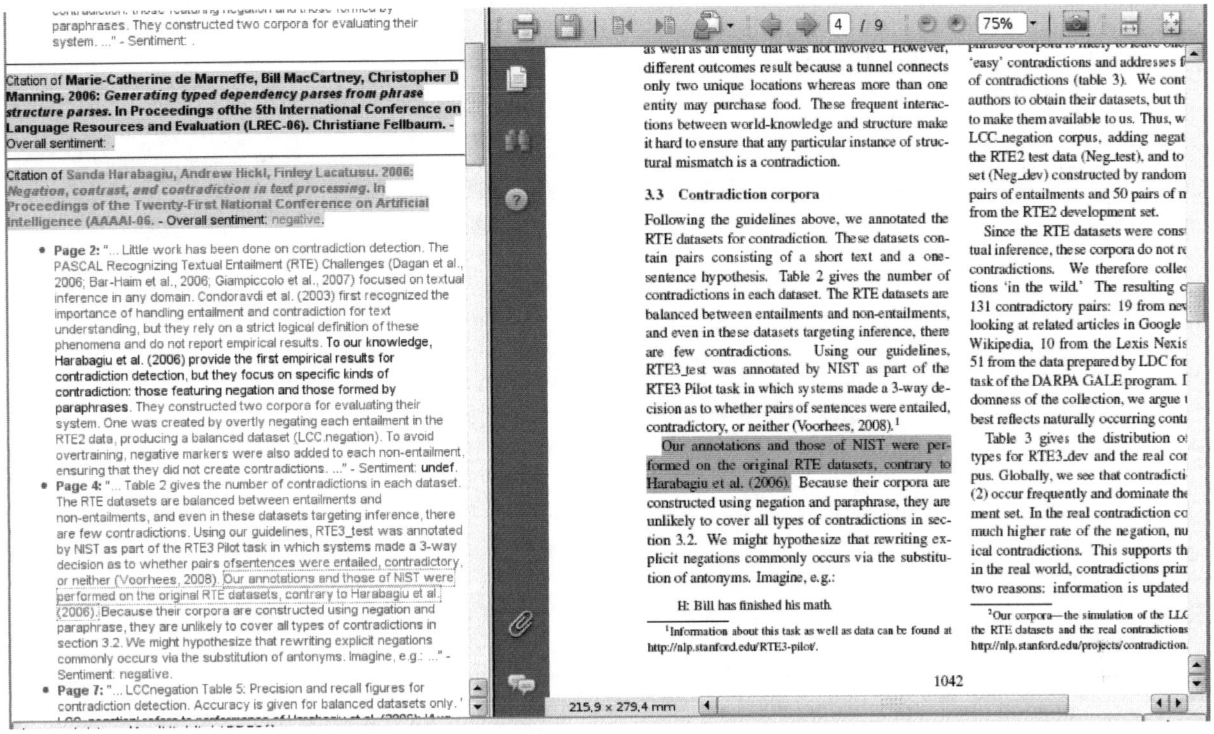

Figure 8: Citation sentence viewer; citation sentence in context on the left, highlighted in PDF on the right when selected on the left

puted citation classifications. In this community application, all citation links in the automatically generated graph could be represented by dashed arrows initially, and users could turn them solid by confirming or correcting the citation type and also adding a comment text.

Line thickness could be increased (up to an appropriate maximum) each time another user confirms a classified citation type. The results could then also be employed for active learning and help to improve the automatic classification procedure.

Acknowledgments

First of all, we are indebted to the anonymous reviewers for their useful, encouraging and detailed comments. Many thanks also to Donia Scott for her feedback on an earlier version of the tool and helpful comments on terminology. We would like to thank Madeline Maher and Boris Fersing for generating and evaluating the citation type data on a subcorpus of the ACL Anthology.

The work described in this paper has been carried out in the context of the project TAKE (Technologies for Advanced Knowledge Extraction), funded under contract 01IW08003 by the German Federal Ministry of Education and Research.

References

Satanjeev Banerjee and Ted Pedersen. 2003. The design, implementation, and use of the ngram statistics package. In *Proceedings of the Fourth International Conference on Intelligent Text Processing and Computational Linguistics*, pages 370–381, Mexico City.

Peter Bergström and E. James Whitehead Jr. 2006. CircleView: Scalable visualization and navigation of citation networks. In *Proceedings of the 2006 Symposium on Interactive Visual Information Collections and Activity IVICA*, College Station, Texas.

Steven Bird, Robert Dale, Bonnie Dorr, Bryan Gibson, Mark Joseph, Min-Yen Kan, Dongwon Lee, Brett Powley, Dragomir Radev, and Yee Fan Tan. 2008. The ACL anthology reference corpus: A reference dataset for bibliographic research. In *Proceedings of the Language Resources and Evaluation Conference (LREC-2008)*, Marrakesh, Morocco.

Lutz Bornmann and Hans-Dieter Daniel. 2008. What do citation counts measure? A review of studies on citing behavior. *Journal of Documentation*, 64(1):45–80. DOI 10.1108/00220410810844150.

Chaomei Chen. 2006. *Information Visualization: Beyond the Horizon*. Springer. 2nd Edition, Chapter 5.

Isaac G. Councill, C. Lee Giles, and Min-Yen Kan. 2008. ParsCit: An open-source CRF reference string parsing package. In *Proceedings of the Language Resources and Evaluation Conference (LREC-2008)*, Marrakesh, Morocco.

Niklas Elmqvist and Philippas Tsigas. 2004. CiteWiz: A tool for the visualization of scientific citation networks. Technical Report CS:2004-05, Department of Computing Science, Chalmers University of Technology and Göteborg University, Göteborg, Sweden.

Eugene Garfield. 1955. Citation indexes for science: A new dimension in documentation through association of ideas. *Science*, 123:108–111.

Eugene Garfield. 1965. Can citation indexing be automated? In Mary Elizabeth Stevens, Vincent E. Giuliano, and Laurence B. Heilprin, editors, *Statistical Association Methods for Mechanical Documentation*. National Bureau of Standards, Washington, DC. NBS Misc. Pub. 269.

Mark Garzone. 1996. Automated classification of citations using linguistic semantic grammars. Master's thesis, Dept. of Computer Science, The University of Western Ontario, Canada.

Vladimir I. Levenshtein. 1966. Binary codes capable of correcting deletions, insertions, and reversals. *Soviet Physics Doklady*, 10(8):707–710.

Robert. E Mercer and Chrysanne Di Marco. 2004. A design methodology for a biomedical literature indexing tool using the rhetoric of science. In Lynette Hirschman and James Pustejovsky, editors, *HLT-NAACL 2004 Workshop: BioLINK 2004, Linking Biological Literature, Ontologies and Databases*, pages 77–84, Boston, Massachusetts, USA.

George A. Miller, Richard Beckwith, Christiane Fellbaum, Derek Gross, and Katherine J. Miller. 1993. Five papers on WordNet. Technical report, Cognitive Science Laboratory, Princeton University.

Quang Vinh Nguyen, Mao Lin Huang, and Simeon Simoff. 2007. Visualization of relational structure among scientific articles. *Advances in Visual Information Systems*, pages 415–425. Springer LNCS 4781, DOI 10.1007/978-3-540-76414-4_40.

David A. Pendlebury. 2009. The use and misuse of journal metrics and other citation indicators. *Archivum Immunologiae et Therapiae Experimentalis*, 57(1):1–11. DOI 10.1007/s00005-009-0008-y.

Dragomir R. Radev, Pradeep Muthukrishnan, and Vahed Qazvinian. 2009. The ACL anthology network corpus. In *Proceedings of the ACL Workshop on Natural Language Processing and Information Retrieval for Digital Libraries*, Singapore.

Ulrich Schäfer, Hans Uszkoreit, Christian Federmann, Torsten Marek, and Yajing Zhang. 2008. Extracting and querying relations in scientific papers. In *Proceedings of the 31st Annual German Conference on Artificial Intelligence, KI 2008*, pages 127–134, Kaiserslautern, Germany. Springer LNAI 5243. DOI 10.1007/978-3-540-85845-4_16.

Simone Teufel, Advaith Siddharthan, and Dan Tidhar. 2006. Automatic classification of citation function. In *Proceedings of the 2006 Conference on Empirical Methods in Natural Language Processing*, pages 103–110, Sydney, Australia.

Grammaticality Judgement in a Word Completion Task

Alfred Renaud[2] and **Fraser Shein**[1,2] and **Vivian Tsang**[1]
[1]Bloorview Kids Rehab
150 Kilgour Road
Toronto, ON M4G 1R8, Canada
[2]Quillsoft Ltd.
2416 Queen Street East
Toronto, ON M2A 1N1, Canada
{arenaud,fshein,vtsang}@bloorview.ca

Abstract

In this paper, we present findings from a human judgement task we conducted on the effectiveness of syntax filtering in a word completion task. Human participants were asked to review a series of incomplete sentences and identify which words from accompanying lists extend the expressions in a grammatically appropriate way. The accompanying word lists were generated by two word completion systems (our own plus a third-party commercial system) where the ungrammatical items were filtered out. Overall, participants agreed more, to a statistically significant degree, with the syntax-filtered systems than with baseline. However, further analysis suggests that syntax filtering alone does not necessarily improve the overall acceptability and usability of the word completion output. Given that word completion is typically employed in applications to aid writing, unlike other NLP tasks, accounting for the role of writer vs. reader becomes critical. Evaluating word completion and, more generally, applications for alternative and augmentative communication (AAC) will be discussed.

1 Introduction

Writers often need help from others to help with spelling and grammar. For persons with physical or learning disabilities, writing can be very stressful because of a greater reliance on the assistance of others. Software tools such as word completion are now commonly used to reduce the physical and cognitive load of completing a word or a sentence and thereby reducing a writer's dependence on others. But can such tools be as effective as a human with adequate linguistic knowledge? While it is hardly possible to completely emulate a human tutor or a communication partner, the purpose of this research is to investigate how much linguistic knowledge is necessary to ensure the usability of word completion. Here, we will focus on the grammaticality of word completion.

1.1 Word Completion

Word completion facilitates text entry by suggesting a list of words that can follow a given linguistic context. If the desired word is in the list, the user can select that word with a mouse click or a keystroke, thereby saving the effort of typing the remaining letters of the word. Otherwise, the user can continue typing while the software continues to display new lists of words based on that input.

For example, consider a user wants to type "That girl by the benches..." After each letter the user manually enters, a system would return a list of potential next words. Say, the next letter the user enters is "w." A system may offer the following choices: a) was, b) were, c) with, d) where, e) wrapped. By suggesting words in any given context, word completion can assist in the composition of well-formed text.

Typical word completion systems suggest words by exploiting *n*-gram Markov statistical models (Bentrup, 1987). These systems probabilistically determine the current word in a sentence given the previous *n*–1 words as context, based on a pre-generated *n*-gram language model derived from a corpus. With *n* typically being of low or-

Proceedings of the NAACL HLT 2010 Workshop on Computational Linguistics and Writing, pages 15–23,
Los Angeles, California, June 2010.

der (two or three, due to sparse data and computational issues), one consequence is that the applicability of suggested words beyond a certain word distance may become somewhat arbitrary. Further design improvements for word completion depend on the user population and the intended use. For example, the demand on the system to have a sophisticated language model may depend on whether the intent is to primarily reduce the physical or cognitive load of entering text. Evaluation approaches can elucidate on design and implementation issues for providing meaningful word choices.

1.2 Evaluation Approaches

A number of studies have been carried out to evaluate the efficacy of word completion systems. Koester (1994) measured *time savings*, which is the reduction in time that the user takes to generate a particular text with the aid of a word completion system compared to the time taken without it. The rationale for this measure is that any word completion system imposes a cognitive load on its users, whereby they now need to 1) change their focus between the target document and the word list display, and possibly between the screen and keyboard; 2) visually scan the word list to decide whether their intended word is present; and 3) select the intended word with the keyboard or mouse. Others have also examined similar visual-cognitive issues of using word completion (e.g., Tam and Wells, 2009). The overall approach implicitly defines a user-centred approach to evaluation by having human subjects simulate the actual writing process (usually in a copying, not writing task). Thus, results depend on the abilities and preferences of individual subjects.

System-based evaluation measures exist, the most common of which is *keystroke savings*. This measures the reduction in the number of keystrokes needed to produce a given text with the aid of a word completion system. Keystroke savings is an important factor for users with physical disabilities who have difficulty working with a keyboard for which it is desirable to keep the number of keystrokes to a minimum. A complementary measure, *completion keystrokes*, determines how quickly a given word is predicted by counting the number of characters required to reach completion. Completion keystrokes differs from keystroke savings in that the latter counts the letters remaining in the word.

In contrast to the previous two measures, both of which measure at the character level, *hit rate* measures at the word level by calculating the ratio of the number of words correctly predicted to the total number of words predicted. Given a sufficiently large lexicon, hit rate can be as high as 100% if every letter of every word is manually entered to its completion. As this can be misleading, hit rate is more typically measured with reference to the number of characters already typed in order to assess the system's demand on the user.

These objective measures address motor load independent of cognitive load. With the exception of time savings, these measures can be benchmarked automatically by simulating the writing process by using existing texts.

A shortcoming of these objective measures is that they focus on the reduction on the user's physical demand by simulating the entering of an already written text, and effectively ignore consideration of word choices other than the unique intended word. In reality, the actual writing process depends also on the quality of the entire group of suggested word choices with respect to the intended content. Renaud (2002) addressed this shortcoming by arguing that the syntactic and semantic relations between words can impact on choice-making at the target word. He introduced two measures, *validity* and *appropriateness*, measuring grammatical consistency and semantic relevance of *all* system output, respectively. The former measure calculates the proportion of a system's suggested words that is syntactically acceptable. The latter focuses on the proportion of relevant output based on lexical and domain semantics. Renaud compared a number of commercial systems and found a positive correlation between the new and existing measures. This finding also lends additional support to Wood's (1996) finding that offering syntactically and semantically appropriate choices improves performance. (Note that the converse may not hold true.)

For the remainder of this paper, we will put our emphasis on the impact of linguistic content (here, grammaticality) on the quality of word completion. The paper is organized as follows. In the next section, we will describe the need to incorporate syntactic information in word completion. In sections 3 and 4, we will describe our human judgement task evaluating the grammaticality of word completion. Based on our analysis, we will return to the evaluation issue in section 5 and discuss how grammaticality alone does not address the larger usability issue of word completion. Here, we propose that the word completion task, unlike traditional NLP tasks, requires both the reader's and writer's perspectives, which impacts the interpretation of our evaluation, and in turn impacts design decisions. In section 6, we will conclude by offering a more inclusive perspective on AAC.

2 The Demand for Syntactic Filtering

As shown earlier, many evaluation methods have focused on 1) the proportion of key-presses normally required during a typing session that the user need not to manually enter and 2) the proportion of text words in a typing session that the system is able correctly to predict. For a user with a learning disability or language difficulties, a greater concern is that all presented words be valid, logical, and free of grammatical errors. Current state-of-the-art systems suffer by suggesting words that are often syntactically implausible while excluding more justifiable but less probable suggestions (cf. our example in section 1). A user may be confused by inappropriate suggestions, even if correct suggestions are also present.

To quantify the importance of syntax in word completion, we compare the average hit rate scores (over all words) with the hit rate scores at points in sentences we consider as syntactically critical (see section 3 for their selection). Nantais et al. (2001) reported an overall hit rate of approximately 56% using bigram word completion after entering the first letter of a word across a large document. However, at the word location where it is crucial to maintain correct syntactic relation with the existing sentence fragment, hit rates are often much lower. In our study situation, the hit rate is at best 39%—these syntactic challenges tend to be semantically contentful and thus present difficulties to human subjects. Likewise, the systems are expected to struggle with them. Without a clear understanding of content specific issues during writing, examining time and keystroke savings alone does not reveal the increased difficulty a user faces at these word positions. We will return to these issues in section 5.

2.1 Building Syntactic Knowledge

Knowledge of syntax can be obtained by first tagging each dictionary word with its part of speech, such as noun or adjective. This information may then be used in either a probabilistic or a symbolic manner. Systems may reason probabilistically by combining tag *n*-gram models, where the part-of-speech tags for the previous *n*–1 words in a sentence are used to predict the tag for the current word, with word *n*-gram models that cue the resulting part(s) of speech to find words proper (Hunnicutt and Carlberger, 2001). Fazly and Hirst (2003) introduced two algorithms for combining tag trigrams with word bigrams. The first algorithm involved conditional independence assumptions between word and tag models, and the second algorithm involved a weighted linear combination of the two models.

A fundamental limitation to this approach is that low-order probabilistic language models can only account for relationships between closely co-located words. Symbolic syntactic prediction guided by a grammar, on the other hand, can deal with long-distance word relationships of arbitrary depth by applying rules that govern how words from syntactic categories can be joined, to assign all sentence words to a category. This approach uses knowledge of English grammar to analyze the structure of the sentence in progress and determine the applicable syntactic categories (e.g., noun, verb), along with other features (e.g., singular, past participle), to which the currently typed/predicted word must belong. In this way a word completion system is able to suggest words that are grammatically consistent with the active sentence fragment.

As such, research closer in nature to our work involves parsers that process the input sentence incrementally as each word is entered. Wood's (1996) augmented phrase-structure grammar showed that symbolic syntactic prediction can improve overall performance when combined with statistical orthographic prediction. McCoy (1998) used the augmented transition network or ATN (Woods, 1970) formalism to find candidate word categories from which to generate word lists. Gustavii and Pettersson (2003) used a chart parser to re-rank, or filter, word lists by grammatical value. These parsing algorithms manipulate some data structure that represents, and imposes ordering on, syntactic constituents of sentences. Recently, we have been developing a syntax module (Renaud et al., 2010) based on an ATN-style parser, which can facilitate both increasing the level of correctness in parses through grammar correction, and modifying the information collected during parsing for a particular application (Newman, 2007). Specifically, this system filters words provided by *n*-gram completion such that the word list only shows words that fit an acceptable grammatical structure. It operates on a longer list of the same frequency-ranked words our core predictor generates. Under this setup, our syntax module can influence the final list shown to the user by demoting implausible words that otherwise would have been displayed and replacing them with plausible words that otherwise would not. Our rationale for using a symbolic vs. a probabilistic parser in word completion is beyond the scope of the current paper.

3 Grammaticality Judgement Experiment

To evaluate the impact of syntactic filtering on word completion, we devised a human judgment task where human subjects were asked to judge the grammatical acceptability of a word offered by word completion software, with or without syntactic filtering. Given a partial sentence and a leading prefix for the next word, word completion software presents a number of choices for the potential next word. Although the goal is to assess the grammaticality of predicted words with or without syntactic filtering, the intent is to assess whether the inclusion of syntactic heuristics in the word completion algorithm improves the quality of word choices.

3.1 Experimental Setup

In our experiment, we compared three different word completion systems: our baseline completion system (WordQ®[*], henceforth "baseline"), our word completion system with syntax filtering ("System B"). We also included a third-party commercial word completion system with syntax filtering built-in (Co:Writer®[†], "System C"). In each system, we inputted a partial sentence plus the leading character for the next word. Each system returned a list of five choices for the potential next word. Our subjects were asked to judge the grammatical acceptability of each word (binary decision: yes or no).

It is worth noting that the more letters are manually inserted, the narrower the search space becomes for the next word. Nantais et al. (2001) suggested that after inserting two characters, the hit rate via automatic means can be as high as 72%; the hit rate for humans is likely much higher. Given that our goal is to examine the grammaticality of word choices and not hit rate, providing only one leading letter allows sufficient ambiguity on what the potential next word is, which in turn allows for a range of grammatical choices for our judgement task.

3.2 Sentence Selection

We selected our test sentences from Canadian news sources (Toronto Star and the Globe and Mail), which are considered reliably grammatical. We chose a total of 138 sentences.[‡] Each sentence was truncated into a fragment containing the first x-1 words and the first character of the xth word, where x ranges from three to ten inclusive. The truncation position x was deliberately selected to include a variety of grammatical challenges.

We divided the sentence fragments into nine types of grammatical challenges: 1) subject-verb agreement; 2) subject-verb agreement in question-asking; 3) subject-verb agreement within a relative clause; 4) appositives; 5) verb sequence (auxiliary verb-main verb agreement); 6) case agreement; 7) non-finite clauses; 8) number agreement; and 9) others.

For example, the sentence "That girl by the benches was in my high school" from section 1.1 can be used to test the system's ability to recognize subject-verb agreement if we truncate the sentence to produce the fragment "That girl by the benches w___." Here, subject-verb agreement should be decided against the subject "girl" and not the (tempting) subject "benches."

[*] http://www.wordq.com; our baseline system uses a bigram language model trained on a corpus of well-edited text.
[†] http://www.donjohnston.com/products/cowriter/index.html

[‡] We did not pick a larger number of sentences due to the time constraint in our experimental setup. The rationale is to avoid over-fatiguing our human subjects (approximately an hour per session). Based on our pilot study, we were able to fit 140 sentences over three one-hour sessions.

After the initial selection process, we reduced our collection to 123 partial sentences. Because the sentences were not evenly distributed across the nine categories, we divided the sentences into three sets such that the frequency distribution of the sentence types was the same for all three sets (41 sentences per set). The three word completion systems were each assigned a different set.[§]

3.3 Grammaticality Judgements

We fed each partial sentence into the corresponding system to produce a word list for grammatical judgement. Recall our example earlier, given five word choices per partial sentence, for each word choice, our subjects were asked to judge its grammatical acceptability (yes or no).

We recruited 14 human subjects, all native speakers of English with a university education. Each subject was presented all 123 sentences covering the three systems, in a paper-based task. The sentence order was randomized and the subjects were unaware of which system produced what list.

Given that each system produced a list of five options for each partial sentence, each subject produced 5×41=205 judgements for each system. There were 14 sets of such judgements in total.

4 Results and Analysis

Our primary objective is to examine the subjects' agreement with the system, and whether the subjects generally agree among themselves. Our rationale is this. If the subjects generally agree with one another, then there is an overall agreement on the perception of grammaticality in word completion. If this is indeed the case, we then need to examine how and why our subjects agree or disagree with the systems. Otherwise, if there is low inter-subject agreement, aside from issues related to the experimental setup, we need to reconsider whether offering grammatical word completion choices is indeed practical and possible.

We first calculated individual participant agreement with the output of each system (i.e., averaged over all participants). The baseline scored 68%. System B scored 72% and System C scored 74%. Thus, an early important result was that syntax assistance in general, independent of particular approach or algorithm, does appear to improve subject agreement in a word completion task. (Note that we treat system C as a black box as we are not privy to its algorithms, which are not published.)

Overall, the grammaticality of a given test word (i.e., averaged over all test words) had an average agreement of 85%, or by 12 of the 14 participants. The percentage agreement for each system was 84% for the baseline, 87% for system B, and 86% for system C. If at least two-thirds of the participants (10 of 14) agreed on the grammaticality of a particular test word, we considered the collective opinion to be consistent for that word and declared a consensus. Participants reached consensus on 77% of the test words for the baseline, 82% of the test words for system B, and 80% of the test words for system C.

Next, we calculated consensus participant agreement for each system. This measure was different from the previous in that we considered only those cases where 10 or more of the 14 participants agreed with one another on the grammaticality of a system's test word and discarded all other cases. In 75% of the consensus cases for the baseline, the subjects agreed with the system (by approving on the grammaticality); in the other 25% of the consensus cases the subjects disagreed with the system. System B scored 78% on the consensus agreement and system C scored 81%.

A repeated-measures analysis of variance (ANOVA) was performed on the data. For both individual and consensus participant agreement, each of Systems B and C outperformed the baseline system (statistically significant, $p<.05$), while the difference between the two systems with syntax awareness was not statistically significant.

To summarize our findings, our subjects generally found the output grammatically more acceptable if syntactic assistance was built in (72% and 74% over 68% in raw participant agreement; 78% and 81% over 75% in consensus agreement). The behaviour of our System B generally was in line with the behaviour of the third-party System C. Finally, the agreement among subjects for all systems was quite high (~85%) and is considered reliable.

[§] We initially to used three different sets, i.e., one set per system, to avoid a sampling "fluke" of different grammatical difficulties/categories. However, for exactly the same reason, we also tested our system using the two sets for the other two systems for ease of comparison. See section 4.1 for details.

4.1 Subject Agreement with Other Systems

To further understand the behaviour of our own system (in contrast to our subjects' judgements), we create two new systems, A' and C' based on the output of the baseline system and the third-party System C. Recall that the sentence set used in each system is mutually exclusive from the set used in another system. Therefore, this setup introduces an additional set of 41 sentences × 5 predicted words × 2 systems = 410 judgements.

Our setup is simple: we feed into our parser each of the sentence fragments for the corresponding system, along with each predicted word originally produced. If our parser accepts the word, the analysis remains unchanged. Otherwise, we count it as a "negative" result, which we explain below.

Consider again our earlier example, "The girl by the benches w___." Say system C' produces the following options: a) was, b) were, c) with, d) where, e) wrapped. We then attempt to generate a partial parse using the partial sentence with each predicted word, i.e., "The girl by the benches was," "The girl by the benches were," and so on. If, for instance, our parser could not generate a parse for "The girl by the benches where," then we would treat the word choice "where" as not approved for the purpose of recalculating subject agreement. So if any subjects had approved its grammaticality (i.e., considered it a grammatical next word), then we counted it as a disagreement (between the parser and the human judge), otherwise, we considered it an agreement.

Consider the following example. One partial sentence for System C was "Japanese farmers immediately pick the shoots which a[m]..." Only 1 of 14 judges agreed with it. System C' also flagged "am" as ungrammatical. Now 13 judges agreed with it.

On the other hand, consider this partial sentence originally from the baseline system, "The reason we are doing these i[nclude]..." where 10 judges said yes but our parser could not generate a parse. In this case, A' scores 4 on agreement.

Overall, A' overrode 10 decisions and scored 71% agreement as a result. That is a 3% improvement over the baseline 68% score. Nine of the 10 reversed consensus in a positive direction and 1 (example above) reversed consensus in a negative direction. In comparison, C' overrode 6 decisions, and scored 76% (2.0% improvement over the original 74%). Five of 6 cases reversed consensus, all in a positive direction. (The other case reversed a non-consensus in a positive direction.) Given that the theoretical maximum agreements for the two systems are 84% and 86% (i.e., regardless of polarity), there is considerable increase in the subject agreement.

It is worth noting that many subjects made the number agreement mistake due to proximity. In the previous example, "The reason we are doing these i[nclude]...", the subjects made the incorrect agreement linking "include" to "these" instead of linking to "the reason." While these cases are not prevalent, this is one reason (among many) that the theoretical maximum agreement is not 100%.

4.2 System's vs. Subjects' Perspective

Although the agreement between the systems and the subjects were high, no system achieved perfect agreement—many words were considered ungrammatical extensions of the partial sentences. We see two possible explanations: 1) the disagreeable output was erroneous; or 2) the disagreeable output was grammatical but judged as ungrammatical under certain conditions.

We manually examined the parse trees of the "disagreeable" cases from our system. Interestingly, in most cases, we found there exists a reasonable parse tree leading to a grammatical sentence. We thus conclude that grammaticality judgements of partial sentences might not completely reflect the underlying improvement of the word completion quality. That is, discrepancies between human and computer judgement need not point to a poor quality syntax filter; instead, it may indicate that the system is exhibiting correct behaviour but simply disagrees with subjects on the particular grammatical cases in question. In such cases, subjects' disagreement with the system does not provide sufficient grounds for making modifications to the system's behaviour. Rather, it is worth examining the factors leading to the subjects' perception of a word as an ungrammatical extension of a partial sentence.

5 Discussion

Overall, our results indicate that our subjects agree with the grammaticality of word completion more when syntactic filtering is used than not.

That said, in light of the disagreeable cases, we believe that the quality of word completion may not be so straightforwardly evaluated.

5.1 Selectional Restriction

Take this example, "The plane carrying the soldiers a___." The next word "are" was unanimously considered ungrammatical by our human judges. Consider the following full sentence version of it: "The plane carrying the soldiers are contemplating is too difficult a task." In this case, the subject is "the plane carrying" (as an activity), the relative clause is "the soldiers are contemplating", and finally, the verb phrase is "is too difficult a task." This sentence may be difficult to interpret but a meaningful interpretation is possible syntactically and semantically.

Consider the following variation, "The political situation the soldiers a___." In this case, it is not difficult to conceive that "are" is a possible next word, as in "The political situation the soldiers are discussing is getting worse." The syntactic construction is [noun phrase] [relative clause] [verb phrase]. Both partial sentences have a potential grammatical parse. Why then is one considered grammatical and the other not?

Sentences that induce midpoint reading difficulties in humans are well known in psycholinguistics and are referred to as garden-path sentences (Frazier, 1978). Reading "the plane carrying the soldiers" induces an expectation in the reader's mind that the sentence is about the plane doing the carrying, and not about the carrying of the plane by the soldiers, leading to a "short circuit" at the word "are."

In linguistics and CL, one aspect of this phenomenon, selectional restriction, has been explored previously (most notably Levin, 1993 and Resnik, 1995). Selectional restriction is defined as the semantics of a verb restricting the type of words and phrases that can occur as its arguments. Essentially, the meaning of the verb makes an impact on what is possible syntactically and semantically. What we observe here is a generalized case where it is no longer only about a verb placing syntactic and semantic restrictions on its surrounding words. Instead, we observe how a word or a number of words influencing the semantic interpretation, and in turn impacting on the perception of grammaticality of the next word (cf. hit rate issues in section 2).

5.2 Evaluation Approach

Although our original intent was to study the grammaticality of word completion, ultimately the question is what impacts on the quality of word completion. It is without a doubt that the grammaticality of the next word suggestions impacts on the perception of the quality of word completion. However, we believe the key hinges on whose perspective of quality is considered, which then becomes a usability issue.

Recall that word completion is designed to aid the writing process. The curious part of our evaluation was that we devised it as a grammaticality judgement task via reading. Is grammaticality different when one is reading vs. writing? We consider this issue in two ways.

Partial Sentences vs. Full Sentences

Let us revisit our garden-path example:

1a. The plane carrying the soldiers a[re]...
1b. The plane carrying the soldiers are contemplating is not that difficult a task.
2a. The political situation the soldiers a[re]...
2b. The political situation the soldiers are losing sleep over is getting worse.

In sentences 1a and 2a, readers have no choice but to judge the grammaticality of "are" based on the existing partial sentence. Depending on the reader's creativity, one may or may not anticipate potential full sentences such as 1b and 2b. In contrast, consider an alternative experimental setup where the readers were offered full sentences such as 1b and 2b and were asked to judge the grammaticality of "are." Given the complexity of the sentences (selectional restriction aside), the readers would have no choice but to consider the existence of a relative clause, which should increase the likelihood of evaluating "are" as a grammatical component of the sentence.

Reading vs. Writing

Now we have observed the potential impact on grammaticality judgements of a potential next word when reading a partial sentence vs. a full sentence. That said, it needs emphasizing that the key issue is to evaluate the quality of a suggested next word given a partial sentence, not grammaticality in complete isolation. When a user uses word completion, he/she is actively engaged in the writing process. No software can truly predict the intent of the writer; the full sentence is waiting to be written and cannot be written a priori.

Consider someone who is in the process of writing the sentence "The plane carrying the soldiers..." Is this writer likely to be debating in his/her head whether the sentence is about the plane that does the carrying or "plane carrying" as an activity? Clearly, the writer's intent is clear to the writer him/herself. In contrast, a sentence may be perfectly grammatical and semantically reasonable, yet a reader may still find it ambiguous and/or difficult to read. In other words, the perception of grammaticality of a next word depends on the task (reading vs. writing). This is *not* to say that our evaluation task is compromised as a result. Despite that the general grammar rules do not change, our reading judgements depending on the context (e.g., partial vs. full sentence) suggests that the reading perspective only provide a partial picture on the quality of output that is intended for a writing task. In our case, higher quality syntactic filtering (e.g., our parser here) may not lead to greater usability.

6 Concluding Remarks

In this paper, we have shown that the quality of word completions depends on the perspective one takes. Considering that AAC is to aid someone in producing content for communication, i.e., for third-party consumption, the reading-writing dichotomy is too serious an issue to ignore. This issue has received some CL attention (Morris, 2004, 2010; Hirst, 2008, 2009) but has not been discussed in the AAC literature (Tsang et al., 2010). The question remains, how do we then evaluate, and more generally, design and use an AAC application?

We believe the issue is far from clear. Take our current focus—grammaticality of word completion. If the form of the content produced is ungrammatical or difficult to read from the perspective of a reader, you risk having the reader misunderstand the writer's intent. However, from the writer's perspective, unless he/she is perceptive of the interpretation problems with his/her potential readers, there is no incentive to produce content as such; the writer can only produce content based on his/her previous linguistic experience.

One may argue that corpus statistics may best capture human linguistic behaviour. For example, hit rate statistics using existing corpora is one such way of assessing the quality of word completion. However, corpora tell only one half of the story—only the writing half is captured, the interpretation issues from the reading side are rarely captured, if at all.

More important, the design of word completion is setup in a way that the task consists of both a reading component and a writing one—the appropriateness of suggested words is assessed by the writer via reading during the writing task. In fact, this is not merely a case of reading vs. writing, but rather, an issue of relevance depending on the linguistic context as well as the user's perception of it. Traditionally, researchers in CL and psycholinguistics have attempted to deal with human processing of linguistic content at various levels (cf. the CUNY Conference on Human Sentence Processing, e.g., Merlo and Stevenson, 2002). However, no computational means is truly privy to the content behind the linguistic form. Content, ultimately, resides in the reader's or the writer's head, i.e., intent. The question remains how best to design AAC to aid someone to communicate this content.

In summary, in our grammaticality judgement task, incorporating syntax in word completion improves the perceived quality of word choices. That said, it is unclear how quality relates to usability. Indeed, the evaluation is far from conclusive in that it only captures the reader's perspective and not the writer's. Currently, we are not aware of the existence of a purely writer-based evaluation for grammaticality of word completion (see Lesher et al., 2002 for one curious attempt). More generally, the reader-writer (or speaker-listener) dichotomy is unexplored in AAC research and should be considered more seriously because communication (as text, speech, or otherwise) involves multiple people producing and consuming content, where the perception of content differs considerably. The challenge of AAC may lie in bridging the gap between production and consumption where communication is neither only about communicating intent nor making interpretations.

Acknowledgments

This project is funded by Quillsoft Ltd. We also wish to thank Jiafei Niu (University of Toronto) for conducting our usability study and Frank Rudzicz (University of Toronto) for providing helpful comments.

References

John Bentrup. 1987. Exploiting Word Frequencies and their Sequential Dependencies. *Proceedings of RESNA 10th Annual Conference*, 121–122.

Afsaneh Fazly and Graeme Hirst. 2003. Testing the Efficacy of Part-of-Speech Information in Word Completion. *Proceedings of the 2003 EACL Workshop on Language Modeling for Text Entry Methods*, 9–16.

Lyn Frazier. 1978. *On Comprehending Sentences: Syntactic Parsing Strategies*. Ph.D. Thesis, University of Connecticut.

Ebba Gustavii and Eva Pettersson. 2003. *A Swedish Grammar for Word Prediction*. Master's Thesis, Department of Linguistics, Uppsala University.

Graeme Hirst. 2008. The Future of Text-Meaning in Computational Linguistics. In *Proceedings of the 11th International Conference on Text, Speech and Dialogue*, 1–9.

Graeme Hirst. 2009. Limitations of the Philosophy of Language Understanding Implicit in Computational Linguistics. In *Proceedings of the Seventh European Conference on Computing and Philosophy*, 108–109.

Sheri Hunnicutt and Johan Carlberger. 2001. Improving Word Prediction Using Markov Models and Heuristic Methods. *Augmentative and Alternative Communication*, 17(4):255–264.

Heidi Koester. 1994. *User Performance with Augmentative Communication Systems: Measurements and Models*. Ph.D. thesis, University of Michigan.

Gregory W. Lesher, Bryan J. Moulton, D. Jeffery Higginbotham, and Brenna Alsofrom. 2002. Limits of Human Word Prediction Performance. In *Proceedings of 2002 CSUN Conference*.

Beth Levin. 1993. *English Verb Classes and Alternations: A Preliminary Investigation*. University of Chicago Press.

Kathleen F. McCoy. 1998. *The Intelligent Word Prediction Project*. University of Delaware. http://ww.asel.udel.edu/nli/nlp/wpredict.html

Paola Merlo and Suzanne Stevenson, Eds. 2002. *The Lexical Basis of Sentence Processing: Formal, Computational and Experimental Issues*. John Benjamins Publishing Company.

Jane Morris. 2004. Readers' Interpretations of Lexical Cohesion in Text. *Conference of the Canadian Association for Information Science*, Winnipeg, Manitoba.

Jane Morris. 2010. Individual Differences in the Interpretation of Text: Implications for Information Science. *Journal of the American Society for Information Science and Technology*, 61(1):141–149.

Tom Nantais, Fraser Shein, and Mattias Johansson. 2001. Efficacy of the word prediction algorithm in WordQ. In *Proceedings of the 2001 RESNA Annual Conference*, 77–79.

Paula S. Newman. 2007. RH: A Retro Hybrid Parser. In *Proceedings of the 2007 NAACL Conference*, Companion, 121–124.

Alfred Renaud. 2002. *Diagnostic Evaluation Measures for Improving Performance of Word Prediction Systems*. Master's Thesis, School of Computer Science, University of Waterloo.

Alfred Renaud, Fraser Shein, and Vivian Tsang. 2010. A Symbolic Approach to Parsing in the Context of Word Completion. In Preparation.

Philip Resnik. 1995. Selectional Constraints: An Information-Theoretic Model and its Computational Realization. *Cognition*, 61:127–125.

Cynthia Tam and David Wells. 2009. Evaluating the Benefits of Displaying Word Prediction Lists on a Personal Digital Assistant at the Keyboard Level. *Assistive Technology*, 21:105–114.

Vivian Tsang and Kelvin Leung. 2010. An Ecological Perspective of Communication With or Without AAC Use. In Preparation.

Matthew Wood. 1996. *Syntactic Pre-Processing in Single-Word Prediction for Disabled People*. Ph.D. Thesis, Department of Computer Science, University of Bristol.

William Woods. 1970. Transition Network Grammars for Natural Language Analysis. *Communications of the ACM*, 13(10):591–606.

The Design of a Proofreading Software Service

Raphael Mudge
Automattic
Washington, DC 20036
raffi@automattic.com

Abstract

Web applications have the opportunity to check spelling, style, and grammar using a software service architecture. A software service authoring aid can offer contextual spell checking, detect real word errors, and avoid poor grammar checker suggestions through the use of large language models. Here we present After the Deadline, an open source authoring aid, used in production on WordPress.com, a blogging platform with over ten million writers. We discuss the benefits of the software service environment and how it affected our choice of algorithms. We summarize our design principles as speed over accuracy, simplicity over complexity, and do what works.

1 Introduction

On the web, tools to check writing lag behind those offered on the desktop. No online word processing suite has a grammar checker yet. Few major web applications offer contextual spell checking. This is a shame because web applications have an opportunity to offer authoring aids that are a generation beyond the non-contextual spell-check most applications offer.

Here we present After the Deadline, a production software service that checks spelling, style, and grammar on WordPress.com[1], one of the most popular blogging platforms. Our system uses a software service architecture. In this paper we discuss how this system works, the trade-offs of the software service environment, and the benefits. We conclude with a discussion of our design principles: speed over accuracy, simplicity over complexity, and do what works.

1.1 What is a Software Service?

A software service (Turner et al., 2003) is an application that runs on a server. Client applications post the expected inputs to the server and receive the output as XML.

Our software service checks spelling, style, and grammar. A client connects to our server, posts the text, and receives the errors and suggestions as XML. Figure 1 shows this process. It is the client's responsibility to display the errors and present the suggestions to the user.

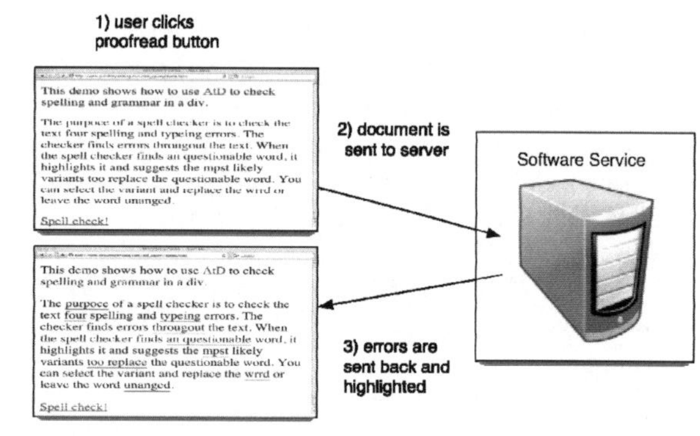

Figure 1. After the Deadline Client/Server Interaction.

[1] An After the Deadline add-on for the Firefox web browser is available. We also provide client libraries for embedding into other applications. See http://www.afterthedeadline.com.

Proceedings of the NAACL HLT 2010 Workshop on Computational Linguistics and Writing, pages 24–32,
Los Angeles, California, June 2010. ©2010 Association for Computational Linguistics

1.2 Applications

One could argue that web browsers should provide spell and grammar check features for their users. Internet Explorer, the most used browser (StatCounter, 2010), offers no checking. Firefox offers spell checking only. Apple's Safari web browser has non-contextual spell and grammar checking. Application developers should not wait for the browsers to catch up. Using a software service architecture, applications can provide the same quality checking to their users regardless of the client they connect with. This is especially relevant as more users begin to use web applications from mobile and tablet devices.

1.3 Benefits

A software service application has the advantage that it can use the complete CPU and memory resources of the server. Clients hoping to offer the same level of proofreading, without a software service, will use more resources on the local system to store and process the language models.

Our system uses large memory-resident language models to offer contextually relevant spelling suggestions, detect real word errors, and automatically find exceptions to our grammar rules.

On disk our language model for English is 165MB uncompressed, 32MB compressed. We use hash tables to allow constant time access to the language model data. In memory our English language model expands to 1GB of RAM. The memory footprint of our language model is too large for a web browser or a mobile client.

A software service also has maintenance advantages. The grammar rules and spell checker dictionary are maintained in one place. Updates to these immediately benefit all clients that use the service.

In this environment, users lose the ability to update their spell checker dictionary directly. To compensate, clients can offer users a way to always ignore errors. Our WordPress plugin allows users to ignore any error. Ignored errors are not highlighted in future checks.

1.4 Operating Requirements

A software service authoring aid must be able to respond to multiple clients using the service at the same time. Our service regularly processes over 100,000 requests a day on a single server.

Our goal is to process one thousand words per second under this load.

Since our system works in the web environment, it must process both text and HTML. We use a regular expression to remove HTML from text sent to the service.

It's important that our service report errors in a way that the client can locate them. The error phrase alone is not enough because suggestions may differ based on the context of the error.

We take a shortcut and provide clients with the text used to match the error and the word that precedes the error phrase. For example, for indefinite article errors, the text used to match the error is the misused article and the word following it. The client searches for this marker word followed by the error text to find the error and present the correct suggestions. This scheme is not perfect, but it simplifies our client and server implementations.

2 Language Model

Our system derives its smarts from observed language use. We construct our language model by counting the number of times we see each sequence of two words in a corpus of text. These sequences are known as bigrams. Our language model is case sensitive.

We trained our bigram language model using text from the Simple English edition of Wikipedia (Wikimedia, 2010), Project Gutenberg (Hart, 2008), and several blogs. We bootstrapped this process by using Wikipedia and Project Gutenberg data. We then evaluated the contents of several blogs looking for low occurrences of commonly misspelled words and real word errors. Blogs that had a low occurrence of errors were then added to our corpus. Our corpus has about 75 million words.

We also store counts for sequences of three words that end or begin with a potentially confused word. A potentially confused word is a word associated with a confusion set (see section 4.1). The real word error detector feature relies on these confusion sets. These counts are known as trigrams. We limit the number of trigrams stored to reduce the memory requirements.

2.1 Functions

Throughout this paper we will use the following functions to refer to our language model.

P(word): This function is the probability of a word. We divide the number of times the word occurs by the total number of words observed in our corpus to calculate the probability of a word.

$P(word_n, word_{n+1})$: This function is the probability of the sequence $word_n\ word_{n+1}$. We divide the number of times the sequence occurs by the total number of words observed in our corpus to calculate the probability of the sequence.

$Pn(word_n|word_{n-1})$: This function is the probability of a word given the previous word. We calculate this with the count of the $word_{n-1}\ word_n$ sequence divided by the count of the occurrences of $word_n$.

$Pp(word_n|word_{n+1})$: This function is the probability of a word given the next word. We use Bayes' Theorem to flip the conditional probability. We calculate this result as: $Pp(word_n|word_{n+1}) = Pn(word_{n+1}|word_n) * P(word_n) / P(word_{n+1})$.

$Pn(word_n|word_{n-1}, word_{n-2})$: This function is the probability of a word given the previous two words. The function is calculated as the count of the $word_{n-2}\ word_{n-1}\ word_n$ sequence divided by the count of the $word_{n-2}\ word_{n-1}$ sequence.

$Pn(word_{n+1}, word_{n+2}|word_n)$: is the probability of a sequence of two words given the word that precedes them. This is calculated as the count of $word_n\ word_{n+1}\ word_{n+2}$ sequence divided by the count of the occurrences of $word_n$.

$Pp(word_n|word_{n+1}, word_{n+2})$: This function is the probability of a word given the next two words. We calculate this result with $Pn(word_{n+1}, word_{n+2}|word_n) * P(word_n) / P(word_{n+1}, word_{n+2})$.

3 Spell Checking

Spell checkers scan a document word by word and follow a three-step process. The first step is to check if the word is in the spell checker's dictionary. If it is, then the word is spelled correctly. The second step is to generate a set of possible suggestions for the word. The final step is to sort these suggestions with the goal of placing the intended word in the first position.

3.1 The Spell Checker Dictionary

The dictionary size is a matter of balance. Too many words and misspelled words will go unnoticed. Too few words and the user will see more false positive suggestions.

We used public domain word-lists (Atkinson, 2008) to create a master word list to generate our spell checker dictionary. We added to this list by analyzing popular blogs for frequently occurring words that were missing from our dictionary. This analysis lets us include new words in our master word list of 760,211 words.

Our spell checker dictionary is the intersection of this master word list and words found in our corpus. We do this to prevent some misspelled words from making it into our spell checker dictionary.

We only allow words that pass a minimal count threshold into our dictionary. We adjust this threshold to keep our dictionary size around 125,000 words.

Threshold	Words	Present Words	Accuracy
1	161,879	233	87.9%
2	116,876	149	87.8%
3	95,910	104	88.0%
4	82,782	72	88.3%
5	73,628	59	88.6%

Table 1. Dictionary Inclusion Threshold.

Table 1 shows the effect of this threshold on the dictionary size, the number of present words from Wikipedia's List of Common Misspellings (Wikipedia, 2009), and the accuracy of a non-contextual version of our spell checker. We will refer to the Wikipedia Common Misspellings list as WPCM through the rest of this paper.

3.2 Generating Suggestions

To generate suggestions our system first considers all words within an edit distance of two. An edit is defined as inserting a letter, deleting a letter, substituting a letter, or transposing two letters (Damerau, 1964).

Consider the word *post*. Here are several words that are within one edit:

cost	substitute p, c	pose	substitute t, e
host	substitute p, h	posit	insert i
most	substitute p, m	posts	insert s
past	substitute o, a	pot	delete e
pest	substitute o, e	pots	transpose s, t
poet	substitute s, e	pout	substitute s, u

The naïve approach to finding words within one edit involves making all possible edits to the misspelled word using our edit operations. You may remove any words that are not in the dictionary to arrive at the final result. Apply the same algorithm to all word and non-word results within one edit of the misspelled word to find all words within two edits.

We store our dictionary as a Trie and generate edits by walking the Trie looking for words that are reachable in a specified number of edits. While this is faster than the naïve approach, generating suggestions is the slowest part of our spell checker. We cache these results in a global least-recently-used cache to mitigate this performance hit.

We find that an edit distance of two is sufficient as 97.3% of the typos in the WPCM list are two edits from the intended word. When no suggestions are available within two edits, we consider suggestions three edits from the typo. 99% of the typos from the WPCM list are within three edits. By doing this we avoid affecting the accuracy of the sorting step in a negative way and make it possible for the system to suggest the correct word for severe typos.

3.3 Sorting Suggestions

The sorting step relies on a score function that accepts a typo and suggestion as parameters. The perfect score function calculates the probability of a suggestion given the misspelled word (Brill and Moore, 2000).

We approximate our scoring function using a neural network. Our neural network is a multilayer perceptron network, implemented as described in Chapter 4 of *Programming Collective Intelligence* (Segaran, 2007). We created a training data set for our spelling corrector by combining misspelled words from the WPCM list with random sentences from Wikipedia.

Our neural network sees each typo ($word_n$) and suggestion pair as several features with values ranging from 0.0 to 1.0. During training, the neural network is presented with examples of suggestions and typos with the expected score. From these examples the neural network converges on an approximation of our score function.

We use the following features to train a neural network to calculate our suggestion scoring function:

editDistance(suggestion, $word_n$)
firstLetterMatch(suggestion, $word_n$)
Pn(suggestion|$word_{n-1}$)
Pp(suggestion|$word_{n+1}$)
P(suggestion)

We calculate the edit distance using the Damerau–Levenshtein algorithm (Wagner and Fischer, 1974). This algorithm recognizes insertions, substitutions, deletions, and transpositions as a single edit. We normalize this value for the neural network by assigning 1.0 to an edit distance of 1 and 0.0 to any other edit distance. We do this to prevent the occasional introduction of a correct word with an edit distance of three from skewing the neural network.

The firstLetterMatch function returns 1.0 when the first letters of the suggestion and the typo match. This is based on the observation that most writers get the first letter correct when attempting to a spell a word. In the WPCM list, this is true for 96.0% of the mistakes. We later realized this corrector performed poorly for errors that swapped the first and second letter (e.g., oyu → you). We then updated this feature to return 1.0 if the first and second letters were swapped.

We also use the contextual fit of the suggestion from the language model. Both the previous and next word are used. Consider the following example:

```
The written wrd.
```

Here *wrd* is a typo for *word*. Now consider two suggestions *word* and *ward*. Both are an edit distance of one from *wrd*. Both words also have a first letter match. *Pp(ward|written)* is 0.00% while *Pp(word|written)* is 0.17%. Context makes the difference in this example.

3.4 Evaluation

To evaluate our spelling corrector we created two testing data sets. We used the typo and word pairs from the WPCM list merged with random sentences from our Project Gutenberg corpus. We also used the typo and word pairs from the ASpell data set (Atkinson, 2002) merged with sentences from the Project Gutenberg corpus.

We measure our accuracy with the method described in Deorowicz and Ciura (2005). For comparison we present their numbers for ASpell and several versions of Microsoft Word along with ours in Tables 2 and 3. We also show the number of misspelled words present in each system's spell checker dictionary.

	Present Words	Accuracy
ASpell (normal)	14	56.9%
MS Word 97	18	59.0%
MS Word 2000	20	62.6%
MS Word 2003	20	62.8%
After the Deadline	53	66.1%

Table 2. Corrector Accuracy: ASpell Data.

	Present Words	Accuracy
ASpell (normal)	44	84.7%
MS Word 97	31	89.0%
MS Word 2000	42	92.5%
MS Word 2003	41	92.6%
After the Deadline	143	92.7%

Table 3. Corrector Accuracy: WPCM Data.

The accuracy number measures both the suggestion generation and sorting steps. As with the referenced experiment, we excluded misspelled entries that existed in the spell checker dictionary. Note that the present words number from Table 1 differs from Table 3 as these experiments were carried out at different times in the development of our technology.

4 Real Word Errors

Spell checkers are unable to detect an error when a typo results in a word contained in the dictionary. These are called real word errors. A good overview of real word error detection and correction is Pedler (2007).

4.1 Confusion Sets

Our real word error detector checks 1,603 words, grouped into 741 confusion sets. A confusion set is two or more words that are often confused for each other (e.g., right and write). Our confusion sets were built by hand using a list of English homophones as a starting point.

4.2 Real Word Error Correction

The real word error detector scans the document finding words associated with a confusion set. For each of these words the real word error detector uses a score function to sort the confusion set. The score function approximates the likelihood of a word given the context. Any words that score higher than the current word are presented to the user as suggestions.

When determining an error, we bias heavily for precision at the expense of recall. We want users to trust the errors when they're presented.

We implement the score function as a neural network. We inserted errors into sentences from our Wikipedia corpus to create a training corpus. The neural network calculates the score function using:

$$Pn(suggestion|word_{n-1})$$
$$Pp(suggestion|word_{n+1})$$
$$Pn(suggestion|word_{n-1}, word_{n-2})$$
$$Pp(suggestion|word_{n+1}, word_{n+2})$$
$$P(suggestion)$$

With the neural network our software is able to consolidate the information from these statistical features. The neural network also gives us a back-off method, as the neural network will deal with situations that have trigrams and those that don't.

While using our system, we've found some words experience a higher false positive rate than others (e.g., to/too). Our approach is to remove these difficult-to-correct words from our confusion sets and use hand-made grammar rules to detect when they are misused.

4.3 Evaluation

We use the dyslexic spelling error corpus from Pedler's PhD thesis (2007) to evaluate the real word error correction ability of our system. 97.8%

of the 835 errors in this corpus are real-word errors.

Our method is to provide all sentences to each evaluated system, accept the first suggestion, and compare the corrected text to the expected answers. For comparison we present numbers for Microsoft Word 2007 Windows, Microsoft Word 2008 on MacOS X, and the MacOS X 10.6 built-in grammar and spell checker. Table 4 shows the results.

Microsoft Word 2008 and the MacOS X built-in proofreading tools do not have the benefit of a statistical technique for real-word error detection. Microsoft Word 2007 has a contextual spell-checking feature.

	Precision	Recall
MS Word 07 - Win	90.0%	40.8%
After the Deadline	89.4%	27.1%
MS Word 08 - Mac	79.7%	17.7%
MacOS X built-in	88.5%	9.3%

Table 4. Real Word Error Correction Performance.

Most grammar checkers (including After the Deadline) use grammar rules to detect common real-word errors (e.g., a/an). Table 4 shows the systems with statistical real-word error correctors are advantageous to users. These systems correct far more errors than those that only rely on a rule-based grammar checker.

5 Grammar and Style Checking

The grammar and style checker works with phrases. Our rule-based grammar checker finds verb and determiner agreement errors, locates some missing prepositions, and flags plural phrases that should indicate possession. The grammar checker also adds to the real-word error detection, using a rule-based approach to detect misused words. The style checker points out complex expressions, redundant phrases, clichés, double negatives, and it flags passive voice and hidden verbs.

Our system prepares text for grammar checking by segmenting the raw text into sentences and words. Each word is tagged with its relevant part-of-speech (adjective, noun, verb, etc.). The system then applies several grammar and style rules to this marked up text looking for matches. Grammar rules consist of regular expressions that match on parts-of-speech, word patterns, and sentence begin and end markers.

Our grammar checker does not do a deep parse of the sentence. This prevents us from writing rules that reference the sentence subject, verb, and object directly. In practice this means we're unable to rewrite passive voice for users and create general rules to catch many subject-verb agreement errors.

Functionally, our grammar and style checker is similar to Language Tool (Naber, 2003) with the exception that it uses the language model to filter suggestions that don't fit the context of the text they replace, similar to work from Microsoft Research (Gamon, et al 2008).

5.1 Text Segmentation

Our text segmentation function uses a rule-based approach similar to Yona (2002) to split raw text into paragraphs, sentences, and words. The segmentation is good enough for most purposes.

Because our sentence segmentation is wrong at times, we do not notify a user when they fail to capitalize the first word in a sentence.

5.2 Part-of-Speech Tagger

A tagger labels each word with its relevant part-of-speech. These labels are called tags. A tag is a hint about the grammatical category of the word. Such tagging allows grammar and style rules to reference all nouns or all verbs rather than having to account for individual words. Our system uses the Penn Tagset (Marcus et al, 1993).

```
The/DT little/JJ dog/NN
laughed/VBD
```

Here we have tagged the sentence *The little dog laughed*. *The* is labeled as a determiner, *little* is an adjective, *dog* is a noun, and *laughed* is a past tense verb.

We can reference little, large, and mean laughing dogs with the pattern *The .*/JJ dog laughed*. Our grammar checker separates phrases and tags with a forward slash character. This is a common convention.

The part-of-speech tagger uses a mixed statistical and rule-based approach. If a word is known and has tags associated with it, the tagger tries to find the tag that maximizes the following probability:

$$P(tag_n|word_n) * P(tag_n|tag_{n-1}, tag_{n-2})$$

For words that are not known, an alternate model containing tag probabilities based on word endings is consulted. This alternate model uses the last three letters of the word. Again the goal is to maximize this probability.

We apply rules from Brill's tagger (Brill, 1995) to fix some cases of known incorrect tagging. Table 5 compares our tagger accuracy for known and unknown words to a probabilistic tagger that maximizes $P(tag_n|word_n)$ only.

Tagger	Known	Unknown
Probability Tagger	91.9%	72.9%
Trigram Tagger	94.0%	76.7%

Table 5. POS Tagger Accuracy.

To train the tagger we created training and testing data sets by running the Stanford POS tagger (Toutanova and Manning, 2000) against the Wikipedia and Project Gutenberg corpus data.

5.3 Rule Engine

It helps to think of a grammar checker as a language for describing phrases. Phrases that match a grammar rule return suggestions that are transforms of the matched phrase.

Some rules are simple string substitutions (e.g., utilized → used). Others are more complex. Consider the following phrase:

```
I wonder if this is your com-
panies way of providing sup-
port?
```

This phrase contains an error. The word companies should be possessive not plural. To create a rule to find this error, we first look at how our system sees it:

```
I/PRP wonder/VBP if/IN
this/DT is/VBZ your/PRP$ com-
panies/NNS way/NN of/IN pro-
viding/VBG support/NN
```

A rule to capture this error is:

```
your .*/NNS .*/NN
```

This rule looks for a phrase that begins with the word *your*, followed by a plural noun, followed by another noun. When this rule matches a phrase, suggestions are generated using a template specified with the rule. The suggestion for this rule is:

```
your \1:possessive \2
```

Suggestions may reference matched words with *\n*, where *n* is the *n*th word starting from zero. This suggestion references the second and third words. It also specifies that the second word should be transformed to possessive form. Our system converts the plural word to a possessive form using the *\1:possessive* transform.

Phrase	Score
your companies way	0.000004%
your company's way	0.000030%

Table 6. Grammar Checker Statistical Filtering.

Before presenting suggestions to the user, our system queries the language model to decide which suggestions fit in the context of the original text.

Rules may specify which context fit function they want to use. The default context fit function is: $Pn(word_n|word_{n-1}) + Pp(word_n|word_{n+1}) > (0.5 \times [Pn(word_n|word_{n-1}) + Pp(word_n|word_{n+1})]) + 0.00001$.

This simple context fit function gets rid of many suggestions. Table 6 shows the scores from our example. Here we see that the suggestion scores nearly ten times higher than the original text.

This statistical filtering is helpful as it relieves the rule developer from the burden of finding exceptions to the rule. Consider the rules to identify the wrong indefinite article:

```
a [aeiouyhAEIOUYH18]\w+
an [^aeiAEIMNRSX8]\w+
```

One uses *a* when the next word has a consonant sound and *an* when it has a vowel sound. Writing rules to capture this is wrought with exceptions. A rule can't capture a sound without hard coding each exception. For this situation we use a context fit function that calculates the statistical fit of the indefinite article with the following word. This saves us from having to manually find exceptions.

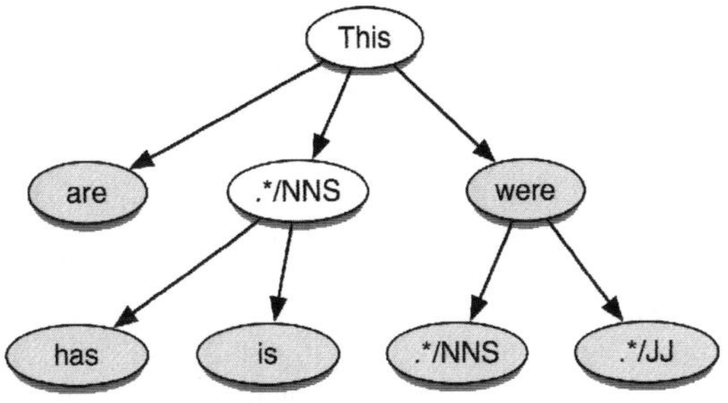

Figure 2. Rule Tree Example.

Each rule describes a phrase one word and tag pattern at a time. For performance reasons, the first token must be a word or part-of-speech tag. No pattern matching is allowed in the first token. We group rules with a common first word or tag into an *n*-ary rule tree. Rules with common pattern elements are grouped together until the word/tag patterns described by the rule diverges from existing patterns. Figure 2 illustrates this.

When evaluating text, our system checks if there is a rule tree associated with the current word or tag. If there is, our system walks the tree looking for the deepest match. Each shaded node in Figure 2 represents a potential match. Associated with each node are suggestions and hints for the statistical checker.

We measure the number of rules in our system by counting the number of nodes that result in a grammar rule match. Figure 2 represents six different grammar rules. Our system has 33,732 rules to check for grammar and style errors.

The capabilities of the grammar checker are limited by our imagination and ability to create new rules. We do not present the precision and recall of the grammar checker, as the coverage of our hand-made rules is not the subject of this paper.

6 Conclusions

Our approach to developing a software service proofreader is summarized with the following principles:

- Speed over accuracy
- Simplicity over complexity
- Do what works

In natural language processing there are many opportunities to choose speed over accuracy. For example, when tagging a sentence one can use a Hidden Markov Model tagger or a simple trigram tagger. In these instances we made the choice to trade accuracy for speed.

When implementing the smarts of our system, we've opted to use simpler algorithms and focus on acquiring more data and increasing the quality of data our system learns from. As others have pointed out (Banko and Brill, 2001), with enough data the complex algorithms with their tricks cease to have an advantage over the simpler methods.

Our real-word error detector is an example of simplicity over complexity. With our simple trigram language model, we were able to correct nearly a quarter of the errors in the dyslexic writer corpus. We could improve the performance of our real-word error corrector simply by adding more confusion sets.

We define "do what works" as favoring mixed strategies for finding and correcting errors. We use both statistical and rule-based methods to detect real word errors and correct grammar mistakes.

Here we've shown a production software service system used for proofreading documents. While designing this system for production we've noted several areas of improvement. We've explained how we implemented a comprehensive proofreading solution using a simple language model and a few neural networks. We've also shown that there are advantages to a software service from the use of large language models.

After the Deadline is available under the GNU General Public License. The code and models are available at http://open.afterthedeadline.com.

Acknowledgements

The author would like to acknowledge the review committee for their questions and suggestions. The author would also like to acknowledge Nikolay Bachiyski, Michael Yoshitaka Erlewine, and Dr. Charles Wallace who offered comments on drafts of this paper.

References

Kevin Atkinson. 2008, Kevin's Wordlist Page. http://wordlist.sourceforge.net/, last accessed: 4 April 2010.

Kevin Atkinson, Spellchecker Test Kernel Results. 2002. http://aspell.net/test/orig/, last accessed: 28 February 2010.

Michele Banko and Eric Brill. 2001. Scaling to very very large corpora for natural language disambiguation. *Proceedings of the 39th Annual Meeting of the Association for Computational Linguistics and the 10th Conference of the European Chapter of the Association for Computational Linguistics*, Toulouse.

Eric Brill. 1995. Transformation-based error-driven learning and natural language processing: a case study in part of speech tagging. *Computational Linguistics*, 21:543–565.

Eric Brill and Robert C. Moore. 2000. An improved error model for noisy channel spelling correction. *Proceedings of the 38th Annual Meeting of the Association for Computational Linguistics*, Hong Kong, pp. 286–293.

Fred J. Damerau. 1964. A technique for computer detection and correction of spelling errors. *Communications of the ACM*, 7(3): 659-664.

Sebastian Deorowicz and Marcin G. Ciura. 2005. Correcting spelling errors by modelling their causes. *International Journal of Applied Mathematics and Computer Science*, 15(2):275–285.

Michael Gamon, Jianfeng Gao, Chris Brockett, Alexander Klementiev, William Dolan, Dmitriy Belenko, and Lucy Vanderwende. 2008. Using Contextual Speller Techniques and Language Modeling for ESL Error Correction. *Proceedings of IJCNLP*, Hyderabad, India, Asia Federation of Natural Language Processing.

Michael Hart. 2008. *Project Gutenberg*. http://www.gutenberg.org/, last accessed: 28 February 2010.

Abby Levenberg. 2007. *Bloom filter and lossy dictionary based language models*. Master of Science Dissertation, School of Informatics, University of Edinburgh.

Mitchell Marcus, Beatrice Santorini, and Maryann Marcinkiewicz. 1993. Building a large annotated corpus of English: the Penn Treebank. *Computational Linguistics*, 19(2).

Daniel Naber. 2003. *A Rule-Based Style and Grammar Checker*. Diplomarbeit Technis Fakultät, Universität Bielefeld, Germany.

Jennifer Pedler. 2007. *Computer Correction of Real-word Spelling Errors in Dyslexic Text*. PhD thesis, Birkbeck, London University.

Segaran, T. 2007 *Programming Collective Intelligence*. First. O'Reilly. pp. 74-85

StatCounter, 2010. *Top 5 Browsers from Feb 09 to Mar 10*. http://gs.statcounter.com/, last accessed: 28 February 2010.

Kristina Toutanova and Christopher D. Manning. 2000. Enriching the Knowledge Sources Used in a Maximum Entropy Part-of-Speech Tagger. *Proceedings of the Joint SIGDAT Conference on Empirical Methods in Natural Language Processing and Very Large Corpora* (EMNLP/VLC-2000), pp. 63-70.

Mark Turner, David Budgen, and Pearl Brereton. 2003. Turning software into a service. *Computer*, 36(10):38–44.

Robert A. Wagner and Michael J. Fischer. 1974. The string-to-string correction problem. *Journal of ACM*, 21(1):168–173.

Wikipedia, 2009. *List of Common Misspellings*. http://en.wikipedia.org/wiki/Wikipedia:Lists_of_common_misspellings, last accessed: 28 February 2010.

Wikimedia Inc. 2010. *Wikimedia Downloads*. http://download.wikipedia.org/, last accessed: 28 February 2010.

Shloma Yona, 2002. *Lingua::EN::Sentence Module*, CPAN. http://search.cpan.org/~shlomoy/Lingua-EN-Sentence-0.25/lib/Lingua/EN/Sentence.pm, last accessed: 28 February 2010.

A Toolkit to Assist L2 Learners Become Independent Writers

John Milton and **Vivying S. Y. Cheng**
Language Center
HKUST, Clear Water Bay
Hong Kong
{lcjohn,vivying}@ust.hk

Abstract

This paper describes a resource-rich toolkit that assists EFL writers take a discovery-based approach to writing accurate and fluent English. The system helps learners identify lexico-grammatical errors by matching patterns gleaned from a very large corpus of learners' texts. Users are guided to appropriate language patterns as they write and revise through online declarative and procedural resources. Even as more robust and fully automatic feedback technologies evolve, comprehensive resource-rich support will remain necessary for second-language (L2) writers who must develop practical life-long language learning strategies. To assist language tutors support novice L2 writers, we have also produced tools that help tutors reinforce their students' independent writing and proofreading strategies. The operation and rationale of this approach have been implemented and evaluated in several Hong Kong universities and secondary schools.

1 Introduction

Proofing technologies for L2 writers have been of interest to the NLP community since the 1970s, and have been subject to critical evaluation since the early 80s (e.g., Frase et al, 1981, Dobrin, 1985). In spite of continued interest in this area (e.g. Vernon, 2000; Foster and Vogel, 2004; Yi et al, 2008; Bender, 2009), computational linguists themselves remain disappointed with the lack of ongoing development of commercially available systems (Wampler, 2002). A more serious problem, from the view of applied linguists, is that enthusiasm for the technology has often resulted in a purely operational approach. The focus on algorithmic solutions to the correction of ill-formed input has frequently overlooked the long-term pedagogical needs of L2 novice writers. The parsing techniques of grammar checkers may reliably flag a subset of L2 errors; however, there is some question as to whether automatically generated prescriptive advice, even when it is reliable, actually helps learner language evolve (Bolt, 1992; Chen, 1997). While machine-generated error identification and correction may be a desirable convenience for casual writers, explicit correction by a machine, or for that matter, a human tutor, appears to be counterproductive in the development of an L2 writer's proficiency (Truscott, 1996; Ferris and Hedgcock, 2005).

The goal of the project described here is to develop a suite of tools that will help novice writers who are learning to write in academic or professional contexts improve the accuracy and fluency of their texts, while also becoming more confident in their long-term command of English. We have developed companion tools to help teachers of writing improve the efficiency and reliability of their feedback, and move L2 novice writers toward life-long independence. The following section outlines some of the limitations of currently available grammar checking software in accomplishing these goals.

2 Limitations of Parsing Technology

Most grammar checking programs use some form of parsing to identify errors. Typically, if a sentence is ungrammatical according to a set of parsing rules, the programs attempt alternate analysis. However, the unconstrained text of L2 learners is

Proceedings of the NAACL HLT 2010 Workshop on Computational Linguistics and Writing, pages 33–41,
Los Angeles, California, June 2010.

difficult to parse. Even more demanding is the ability of software (or, very often, human tutors) to suggest a 'correct' version that reflects the writer's intention. This requires semantic disambiguation well beyond our current ontology or technology.

The difficulties in parsing natural language are compounded in the case of interlanguage (Schneider and McCoy, 1998). Parsers generally are based on theoretical models of how grammatical sentences of the target language should be constructed. This approach is especially ineffective for cases where the speakers' first language is linguistically remote from the target language. For example, the current version of the parser-based grammar checker in Microsoft Word sacrifices a low rate of recall for a relatively high rate of precision in the analysis of Chinese speakers' English texts. That is, it displays few flagged errors compared to the total number of errors actually occurring in a text, a necessary trade-off resulting from the need to reduce distracting false positives. This is understandable since the rates of recall and precision for various grammatical constituents are inconsistent, and the numbers of false positives are not easily reduced across all types of grammatical constructions.

The insufficient, but nevertheless often still inaccurate, and frequently non-existent, advice of these programs is easily demonstrated. Following are a few common sentence-level errors produced by Chinese-speaking novice writers, and the comments generated by the Microsoft Word grammar checker:

1.*It worth studying hard.*
[Advice: Fragment (consider revising)]
2.*I born in Hong Kong.*
[Advice: substitute *I bore / I had born / I have born*]
3.*There have three students there.*
[Error not flagged]

These errors are typical examples of learners' attempts to map Chinese syntax on English constructions (treating 'worth', which functions here as a preposition[1], as a verb, forcing the passive verb 'born' into an active construction, and blending the verbs 'be' and 'have' into one form, as their equivalents are in Chinese). The first comment is unhelpful; all options in the second set of suggestions are, bizarrely, further from Standard English than the student's original text, and the third sentence passes without comment.

In addition to its general unreliability for L2 writers, grammar/style-checking software has been censured for giving overly narrow and prescriptive advice (Pennington, 1992), for compounding the already constrained nature of L2 production (Chapelle, 2001) and for otherwise abusing the tenets of good pedagogy (McGee and Ericsson, 2002). Even if the reliability of parsing technology can be significantly enhanced, much of the composition research of the last fifty years has argued against imposing corrections on the texts of novice writers. Current theories of language pedagogy promote learner independence and discourage direct correction by tutors. In light of the limitations of writing software, reliance on a deus ex machina for correction is hardly a desirable alternative to dependence on a language tutor.

A more principled, and ultimately more valid, role for language tools in supporting L2 novice writers is to enable them to test their evolving hypotheses of the L2. This should free the human tutor in an academic context to act as a guide, ensuring that these hypotheses evolve.

3 Assisting L2 Writers become Independent

Our objective has been to develop a program that avoids machine-generated prescription, while still helping L2 writers identify common grammatical, lexical and style errors. Instead of proscribing usage and preempting users' choices, we expose L2 writers to authentic language and help them become aware of the differences between their interlanguage and the particular L2 genre they are attempting to produce.

Unlike typical grammar checkers, our program does not appropriate the embryonic text of novice writers. Many of these learners will spend much of their professional life writing in the L2, and they need to develop independence. While not explicitly correcting lexico-grammatical errors, we aim to sensitize learners to common errors, without relying on a generic parser.

[1] The tendency of most dictionaries to label '*worth*' as an adjective, regardless of its function in the sentence, may compound the confusion for speakers of Chinese, who often confuse adjective and noun forms and functions.

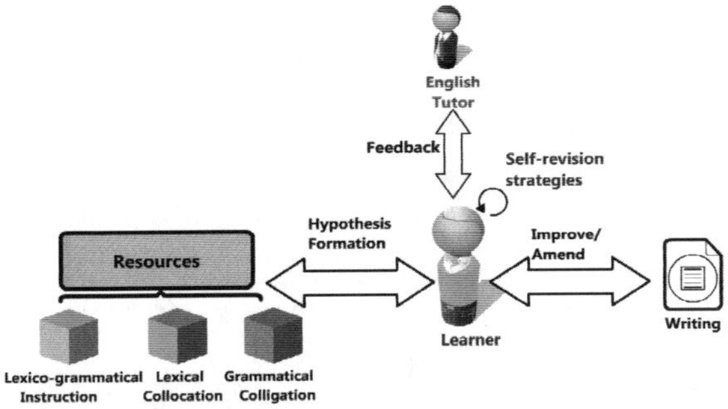

Figure 1: A discovery-based model of the writing process.

Figure 1 illustrates our model of a discovery-based approach for L2 writers. During the writing process, learners can consult resources that provide information on problematic L2 grammatical structures, as well as the semantic and collocational properties of L2 lexis. Users are guided through a discovery process that helps them become responsible for their own writing, thus reducing the burden on both software and human tutors to identify and correct errors. The role of the software, and of the human tutor, is to assist the writer express meaning in an acceptable manner, rather than explicitly to interpret the writer's text.

Our approach allows L2 writers to improve in two fundamentally different ways: through didactic explanations and via an inductive/procedural approach. They can choose either method or a combination, depending on the nature of the language problem and each user's learning style (e.g., their extent of 'field dependence', see Witkin et al., 1977).

The program 'Check My Words' (Figure 2) gives L2 novice writers access to interactive explanations of common structural and lexical errors from an Internet grammar as they write. These explanations are based on an analysis of a large L2 corpus consisting of millions of words of the writing of Chinese speakers, from which a typology of misused, and blatantly underused or overused lexical and structural patterns, was extracted (e.g., Milton, 2001). Hundreds of problematic words and patterns in a learner's text are explained. This is the kind of didactic, deductive advice that a good textbook might provide, except that there are few textbooks targeted directly at the EFL learning difficulties of speakers of particular L1s, and this internet grammar is embellished with interactive multimedia: it is fun to use.

Secondly, the program enables learners to discover how the language they are struggling to use is formulated in relevant, professionally written texts. They have a choice of search engines that they can use to look up words in context. Together, these search engines address many of the problems learners encounter in choosing words, forms and constructions. This inductive, procedural access to writing models, combined with the feedback tutors can provide via companion tools, greatly increases the amount of positive and negative evidence about the L2 available to the novice writer—support that researchers of applied linguistics believe promotes language acquisition (e.g., Trahey and White, 1993, Doughty and Varela, 1998).

In addition to helping learners become more confident, responsible, and independent in selecting language that is both accurate and appropriate to their purposes, this approach helps relieve language tutors of the need to act as proofreading slaves. When learners are given the tools to attend to form, taught how to use the tools, and held accountable for their own progress, teachers can share more of the burden of responsibility for learning with their students. This approach reduces the need to impose corrections, either by human or machine intervention. The next section explains this procedure in more detail.

4 Promoting language awareness

'Check My Words' is designed to encourage learners of English become aware of the role of lexis, forms, and functions in the L2, and to self-correct. Errors in the L2 writing of Chinese speakers have been analyzed and compiled into an online grammar guide mapped to the user's word processor so that problematic words and structures can be queried during the writing process to determine if they are misused in the writer's document.

An example is one of the interlanguage patterns we noted earlier: 'It worth studying hard.' In such cases, where the error is easily captured as a lexical pattern ('worth' occurring without the verb 'be'), the program highlights the pattern, and the user then presses a 'Check' button to see possible errors, with the most probable error highlighted (Figure 3). The user selects a link to consult the English Grammar Guide (EGG).

Figure 2: The *Check My Words* toolbar for EFL learners.

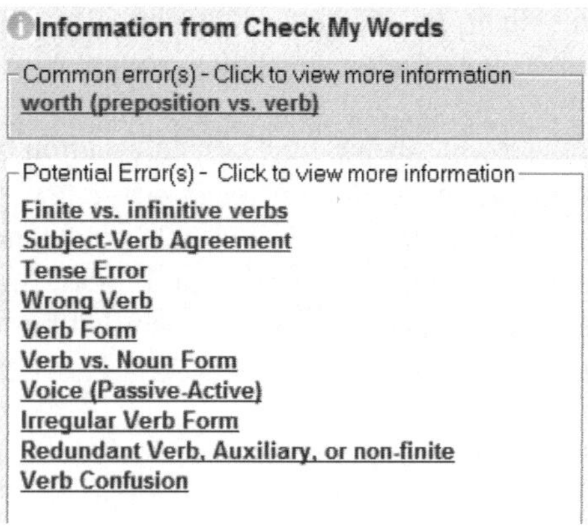

Figure 3: The type of prompt that appears when a learner 'checks' a highlighted expression.

Explanations in the EGG are accompanied by examples and a mini-test. Interesting multimedia resources are also used to illustrate the explanation. For example, in Figure 4, the use of the word 'worth' is exemplified in an advertisement that sells its products with the rationalization that 'you're worth it'.

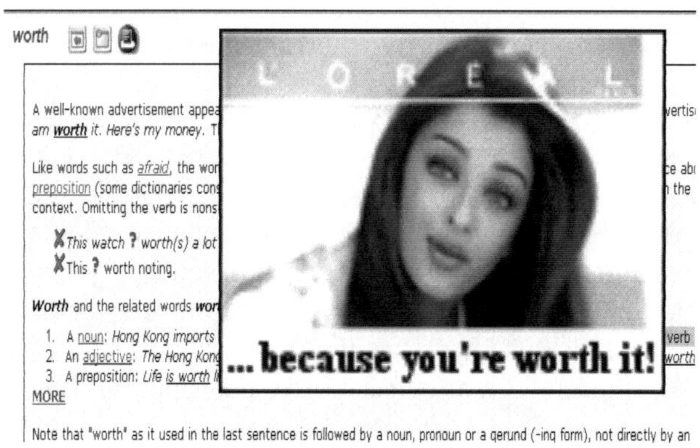

Figure 4: An explanatory fragment of the word 'worth' from the English Grammar Guide.

Over 500 lexico-grammatical errors are indexed, based on a comprehensive analysis of a corpus of the learners' texts. Figure 5 illustrates a cartoon conversation addressing another common error in this interlanguage—the blending of the verb and adjective functions of 'concern' (e.g., 'I concern about…').

Figure 5: An explanatory fragment of the word 'concern' from the *English Grammar Guide.*

In addition to an online descriptive grammar, the program points users to procedural/inductive resources—online lookup engines—where they can explore the contextual properties of difficult L2 patterns and retrieve collocates of any word or pattern.

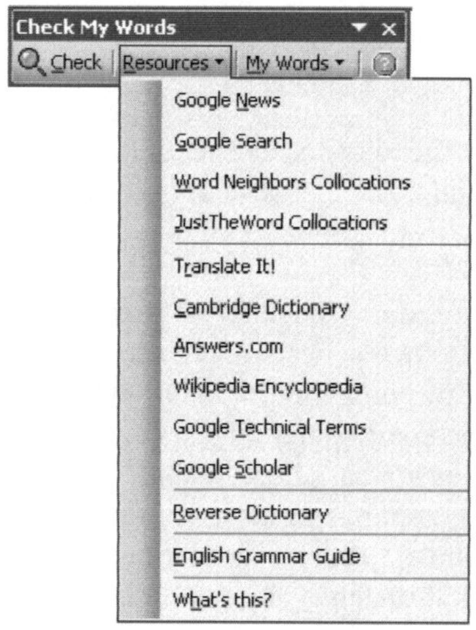

Figure 6: The pull-down list of resources on the *Check My Words* toolbar.

Users choose one of these resources from the Check My Words toolbar (Figure 6), and the program generates appropriate search syntax for each lookup resource (a Google search of the web, news or scholarly articles, or via our own lookup engine, 'Word Neighbors'). These resources provide 'snapshots' of the word or structure in context, which is especially useful for learners who have not read widely in the L2. Word Neighbors displays the collocational properties of words and phrases in selected, professionally written texts, and provides learners the opportunity to explore the relationship between their own output and L2 target forms. Users are guided in looking up words and expressions in Word Neighbors via the dialogue shown in Figure 7.

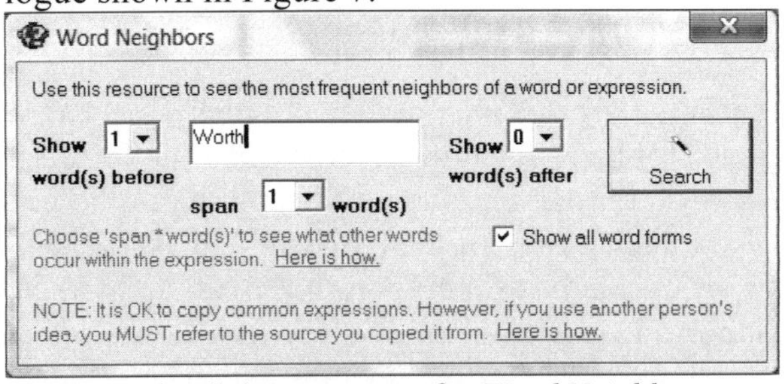

Figure 7: The dialogue prompt for *Word Neighbors.*

The features of Word Neighbors' can be demonstrated by again exploring the sample error: It worth studying hard. Figure 8 displays the word worth as the target word. The search parameters are set by default to display missing words and to suggest alternatives for malformed words. Word Neighbors also displays patterns as they occur in various genres. The parameters Show X words before/after allow users to select the number of words to be shown before or after the target word. The Span X word(s) drop-down enables the user to investigate possible missing or redundant words in a phrase, and the Show all word forms checkbox enables users to display all forms of a word.

The first screen from the Word Neighbors search result (Figure 8) shows all classes2 of the target word and, in this case, the classes that normally precede that word. The user has empirical evidence that worth is usually a preposition preceded by a copula verb. Clicking Show results displays specific instances of this pattern (Figure 9). Clicking See contexts then displays sentences and paragraphs containing the words (Figure 10).

The difference between our approach to error correction and that of systems that rely on automatic detection is well illustrated by preposition errors. Chodorow et al (2007), for example, discuss a method for detecting preposition errors that they report achieves a precision of 0.8 and a recall of 0.3.

[2] Texts are tagged with CLAWS (Garside and Smith, 1997).

Patterns/Words			Frequency
VERB + PREP:	e.g. "is worth"	Show results	6193
ADV + PREP:	e.g. "not worth"	Show results	2602
NOUN + PREP:	e.g. "deal worth"	Show results	2214
PRON + PREP:	e.g. "it worth"	Show results	538
CONJ + PREP:	e.g. "and worth"	Show results	152
DET + PREP:	e.g. "all worth"	Show results	111
ADJ + PREP:	e.g. "better worth"	Show results	30
PREP + PREP:	e.g. "as worth"	Show results	5
VERB + ADJ:	e.g. "is worthy"	Show results	1503
DET + ADJ:	e.g. "a worthy"	Show results	1119
ADV + ADJ:	e.g. "not worthy"	Show results	1079
CONJ + ADJ:	e.g. "and worthy"	Show results	385
NOUN + ADJ:	e.g. "areas worthy"	Show results	331
PRON + ADJ:	e.g. "it worthwhile"	Show results	328
PREP + ADJ:	e.g. "of worthwhile"	Show results	154
ADJ + ADJ:	e.g. "only worthwhile"	Show results	87
NOUN + NOUN:	e.g. "pounds worth"	Show results	1174

Figure 8: *Word Neighbors* displays search result of the word '*worth*' in different word class patterns

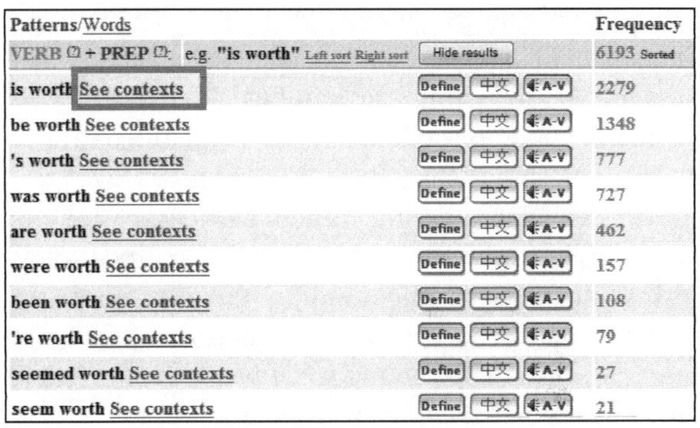

Patterns/Words		Frequency
VERB + PREP: e.g. "is worth" Left sort Right sort	Hide results	6193 Sorted
is worth See contexts	Define 中文 A-V	2279
be worth See contexts	Define 中文 A-V	1348
's worth See contexts	Define 中文 A-V	777
was worth See contexts	Define 中文 A-V	727
are worth See contexts	Define 中文 A-V	462
were worth See contexts	Define 中文 A-V	157
been worth See contexts	Define 中文 A-V	108
're worth See contexts	Define 中文 A-V	79
seemed worth See contexts	Define 中文 A-V	27
seem worth See contexts	Define 中文 A-V	21

Figure 9: *Word Neighbors* displays the search result for the pattern VERB + PREP.

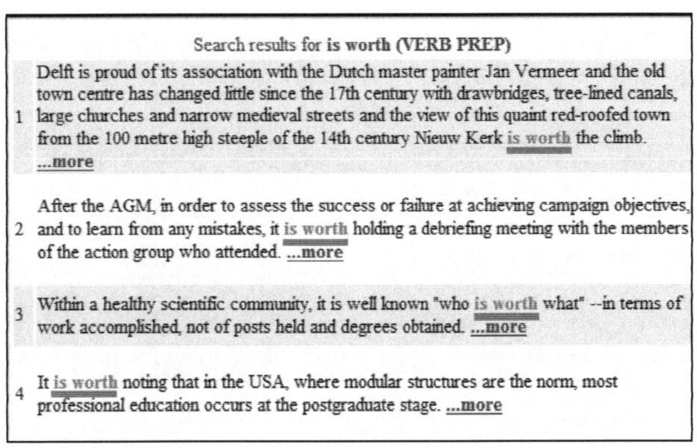

Search results for **is worth (VERB PREP)**

1 Delft is proud of its association with the Dutch master painter Jan Vermeer and the old town centre has changed little since the 17th century with drawbridges, tree-lined canals, large churches and narrow medieval streets and the view of this quaint red-roofed town from the 100 metre high steeple of the 14th century Nieuw Kerk is worth the climb. ...more

2 After the AGM, in order to assess the success or failure at achieving campaign objectives, and to learn from any mistakes, it is worth holding a debriefing meeting with the members of the action group who attended. ...more

3 Within a healthy scientific community, it is well known "who is worth what" --in terms of work accomplished, not of posts held and degrees obtained. ...more

4 It is worth noting that in the USA, where modular structures are the norm, most professional education occurs at the postgraduate stage. ...more

Figure 10: *Word Neighbors* displays sentences containing the pattern *'is worth'*.

While this type of ambitious scientific research is important and interesting, it is still of limited use by non-native writers. We have not attempted to flag preposition errors unless they are invariable associated with a frequently misused lexical pattern (e.g., 'They demanded for more time.'). Instead, the novice writer is encouraged to use a resource such as Word Neighbors to look up the typical patterns of prepositions. These errors lend themselves well to such a pattern-matching approach. If we take this error as an example, the user has only to highlight the words surrounding the preposition, and look up the pattern 'demanded * more'. The program ellipts the preposition and looks for a span of three words, resulting in the display in Figure 11.

Concordance-type tools such as Word Neighbors provide authentic information about the patterns of language, but the L2 writer must often decide which context is appropriate for a particular case. Dialogue boxes and tutorials give learners guidance with this discovery-based learning approach. Supporting pedagogical materials that teachers using these tools have developed allow learners to practice correcting sentence level errors. The materials are aimed particularly at increasing the learners' awareness of collocational restrictions and at encouraging them to look up collocational properties. The materials have been integrated into EFL courses at several Hong Kong universities and secondary schools.

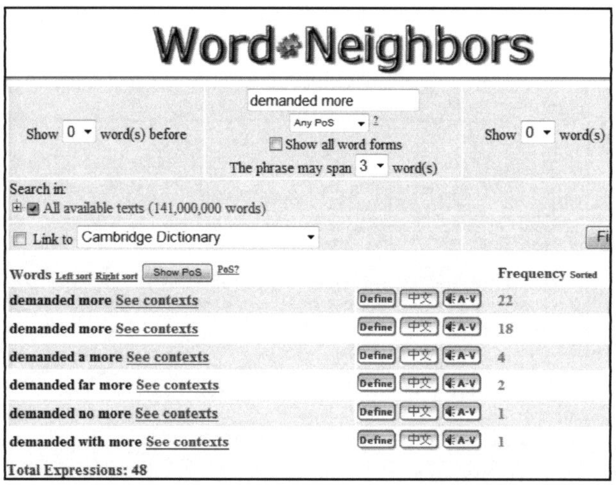

Figure 11: *Word Neighbors* displays the patterns of '*demanded * more*'.

We have found that in institutional contexts where novice writers may have learned to rely completely on teacher feedback for correction, simply putting tools in students' hands is not enough. In the next section, we describe companion tools that enable teachers to prompt their students to notice particular errors and reformulate their sentences without the teacher's explicit correction.

5 Resource-rich Feedback

Teachers of academic written English face enormous problems when they, rather than the learners themselves, bear the burden for improving the accuracy and fluency of their students' texts. Teachers are typically called upon to provide individual support to large numbers of students who are often at various levels of acquisition and who have a wide range of motivational drives and individual needs. These quantitative demands, together with the complexity of understanding and reformulating the texts of novice writers, limit the effectiveness of any feedback a teacher can provide. In addition, teachers often find themselves repeatedly identifying and correcting errors that they have pointed out many times before. This is especially discouraging when the errors reoccur in the same student's texts.

This was the impetus for the design of Mark My Words, a companion to the students' version, Check My Words. Like Check My Words, it installs as a toolbar in Microsoft Word (Figure 12). Teachers can use this tool to insert 'resource rich' comments in students' texts (e.g., Milton, 2006). These comments include links to the resources available from the students' Check My Words toolbar. Students can be held accountable for reformulating their own texts using the same resources they themselves have available during the writing process.

The following steps illustrate the process a teacher might use when responding to a student's text. This procedure is ideally employed after the student has completed at least one draft and followed a revision process similar to that outlined in the previous section. Let's assume that a student has submitted a text containing the error illustrated previously ('It worth studying.').

Teachers have a variety of options in commenting on a text, depending on how explicit they want to be. When the teacher wants to bring an error to

Figure 12: The *Mark My Words* toolbar for tutors of English.

the student's attention, the teacher puts the cursor on the word or highlights a phrase and clicks a Mark button. The program attempts to identify the error based on simple heuristics (e.g., identifying the POS and any pattern that matches a mal-rule), and dialogues such as the following one presented in figure 13 are available.

The 'Topic' and 'Hint' text boxes contain boilerplate comments that the teacher customizes as desired. The teacher can accept the default suggestions or select a resource or search engine and set parameters to display the Standard English lexical pattern. The English Grammar Guide link, online dictionary, and Word Neighbors are selected in this example. These links then appear in the student's text. These links reinforce the student's familiarity with the resources, encouraging students to use the resources to revise their texts.

The student has only to 'mouse over' the teacher's initials to see each 'resource rich' comment, and can click to open the resource. In the example illustrated in Figure 14, three resources are available: usage explanations (the 'Click here for more advice and practice' link points to the relevant page of the online English Grammar Guide), definitions (Cambridge Dictionary), and collocational patterns (Word Neighbors).

Teachers can comment on repeated errors of the same type by clicking a 'Copy Comment' button, although usually it is not necessary (nor advisable) to highlight every error. Current feedback pedagogy suggests that, rather than highlighting all errors, it is more effective to draw students' attention to a subset of errors. In addition to comments covering the most distracting and disruptive types of sentence level errors, the Mark My Words program lists many other comments covering formatting, organization, style, content, and logic. Teachers can easily add more comments, and customize and associate these with any concept or pattern in a student's text, and these in turn with any online resources. By having students concentrate on structures and lexis that are particularly difficult for each individual, we can more reasonably expect L2 novice writers to learn to identify and revise these problems themselves.

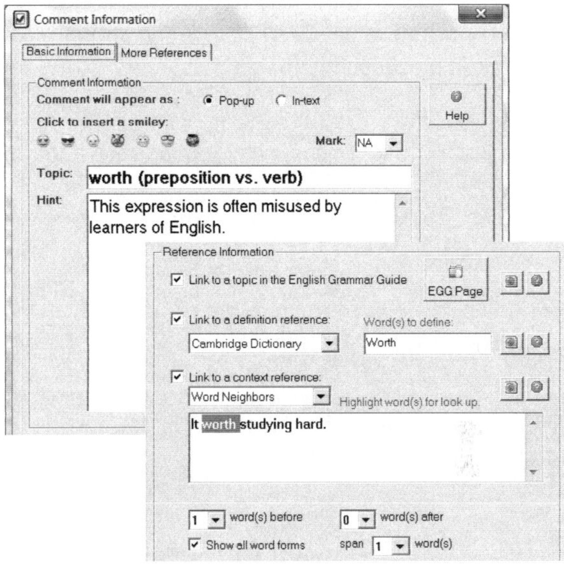

Figure 13: dialogue boxes that allow teachers to customize comments.

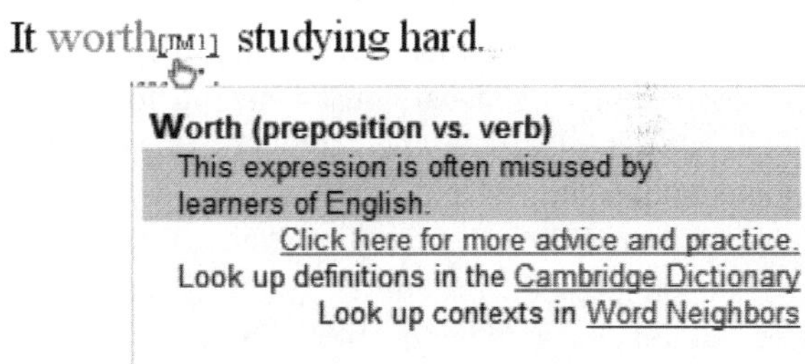

Figure 14: a comment from *Mark My Words*.

The Mark My Words program retains a database of comments made on previous assignments so that a teacher knows whether a student has had attention drawn to particular lexical and structural problems. At the bottom of each text, teachers can generate a 'Comments Table' that summarizes the comments (Figure 15). This allows teachers to maintain a record of comments given to particular students. These comments and error logs are permanently available for students and teachers to refer to as prompts for each subsequent draft and revision.

This procedure does not necessarily replace classroom instruction or individual consultation. However, by encouraging EFL learners to use such resources, and demonstrating their usefulness through instruction and as part of the feedback process, we can equip learners to proofread for themselves, and help them assume responsibility for becoming independent writers.

Comments Summary

Description	Category	Instances	References	Value	Running Total
Unclear/Awkward	Comments	3	[MMW2] [MMW4] [MMW7]	-1 -1 -1	-3
Singular-Plural Form	Singular-plural	3	[MMW5] [MMW6] [MMW9]	-1 -1 -1	-6
Wrong Verb	Wrong / Unclear Word(s)	2	[MMW1] [MMW10]	-1 -1	-8
Redundant Word(s)	Redundant	2	[MMW3] [MMW8]	-1 0	-9
Punctuation	Formatting	2	[MMW12] [MMW13]	-1 -1	-11
Word Order Error	Word Order	1	[MMW11]	0	-11
Wrong or Unclear Noun/ Pronoun	Wrong / Unclear Word(s)	1	[MMW14]	-1	-12

Any scores in this table (under VALUE and RUNNING TOTAL) are for your information.
Your teacher may or may not use these scores in calculating your final grade for this assignment.

Figure 15: a summary of comments from *Mark My Words*.

6 Implementation and Assessment

The tools and techniques described above have been designed with the needs of intermediate and advanced EFL learners in mind—especially Chinese-speaking secondary and tertiary students. This approach meets many of the requirements laid out for corpus-based language learning tools (e.g., Ghadessy et al, 2001 and Romer, 2006). Other work in this area (e.g., Gaskell and Cobb, 2004) has illustrated the promise that such methods have for enabling teachers to guide students in accessing and understanding the discrepancy between their language patterns and those of Standard English.

The programs have been integrated into EFL courses at several Hong Kong universities and secondary schools and continue to undergo refinements based on user feedback. A comprehensive evaluation of students' and teachers' reactions to the programs emphasizes the need for training and pedagogical materials that support teachers and students: a number of genre-specific writing syllabuses (e.g., lab-report writing) are being built around the use of the programs.

Although our main aim is not to identify all errors or prescribe correction, the ability of the Check My Words program to identify the lexico-grammatical errors of a specific cohort of L2 writers (Chinese speakers of English) is steadily improving. We maintain an 'Assignment Management System', through which students and teachers exchange electronic documents. This system enables us to collect user-generated knowledge in the form of common errors in the L2 writing of this cohort of users, as well as errors tagged by their language teachers. Students who use the Check My Words program currently submit approximately 1 million words per month, and teachers tag about 15,000 errors in these texts monthly, using the Mark My Words program. We are able to mine these texts for mal-rules and for the usage marked by their teachers, and we can use the corpus as an iterative test bed for error checking.

A quantitative analysis of about a million words of the re-drafted texts of students who have used the program, and another million words of those who did not use the program during composition show significant improvements in accuracy and fluency of those who used the program. Students who follow this process tend to use a wider range of language formulae and, as well as gaining confidence in using the tools to check lexis and structures, they more successfully attempt grammatical structures normally avoided in the novice L2 writing of speakers of Chinese (such as modality and subordination). In surveys, the L2 novice writers report that they find the programs 'very useful'. Teachers report that students who used the program as a proofreading aid were able to self-correct more reliably than students who did not use the program.

However, although the technical infrastructure of Hong Kong schools and universities can easily accommodate these programs (students and teachers generally have access to good computer facilities), the adoption of this method of feedback by teachers has been slow. Examination-driven teaching practices emphasize teacher-centered methods, and teachers have little incentive to encourage students in independent learning and discovery-based writing. Nevertheless, most teachers who try this method quickly become proficient and embrace it, recognizing that it can help transfer the burden for proofreading to their students. They appreciate being able to customize and share comments, and avoid explicit correction, while still assisting students and holding them accountable for conveying meaning in an acceptable manner and in their own words.

7 Conclusion

The programs described in this paper demonstrate techniques that can help L2 writers acquire accuracy and fluency in written English and develop life-long writing habits in the L2. The approach takes advantage of online resources to help students and teachers shift from a machine- or teacher-centered pedagogy to one that puts the L2 writer at the center of the writing process by making the learner accountable, and ultimately more confident and independent. The Check My Words and Mark My Words programs described in this paper are available from http://mywords.ust.hk/.

References

E. M. Bender. 2009. Linguistically Naïve!=Language Independent: Why NLP Needs Linguistic Typology. *Proceedings of the EACL 2009 Workshop on the Interaction between Linguistics and Computational Linguistics: Virtuous, Vicious or Vacuous?* Athens, Greece, 26–32.

P. Bolt. 1992. An evaluation of grammar-checking programs as self-help learning aids for learners of English as a foreign language. *Computer Assisted Learning*, 5(1–2):49–9.

C. Chapelle. 2001. *Computer Applications in Second Language Acquisition: Foundations for Teaching, Testing, and Research*. Cambridge, UK: Cambridge University Press.

J. F. Chen. 1997. Computer generated error feedback and the writing process. *TESL-EJ Teaching English as a second Foreign Language*, 2(3).

M. Chodorow, J. Tetreault, and N.-R. Han. 2007. Detection of grammatical errors involving prepositions. *Proceedings of the Fourth ACL-SIGSEM Workshop on Prepositions*, Prague, Czech Republic: Association for Computational Linguistics, 25–30.

D. N. Dobrin. 1985. Style analyzers once more. *Computers and Composition*, 3:22–32.

D. Ferris. and J. S. Hedgcock. 2005. *Teaching ESL Composition: Purpose, Process, and Practice* (2nd ed.) Mahwah: Lawrence Erlbaum Associates.

J. Foster. and J. Vogel. 2004. Parsing Ill-Formed Text Using an Error Grammar. *Artificial Intelligence Review*, 21(3-4):269–291.

L. T. Frase, N. H. Macdonald, P. S. Gingrich, S. A. Keenan and J. L. Collymore, 1981. Computer aids for text assessment and writing instruction, *NSPI Journal*, 21.

D. Gaskell, and T. Cobb. 2004. Can learners use concordance feedback for writing errors? *System*, 32(3): 301–319.

M. Ghadessy, A. Henry, and R. Roseberry, (eds.). 2001. *Small Corpus Studies and ELT: Theory and Practice*, John Benjamins.

R. Garside, and N. Smith. 1997. A hybrid grammatical tagger: CLAWS4, In R. Garside, G. Leech and A. McEnery. (eds.) *Corpus Annotation: Linguistic Information from Computer Text Corpora*. Longman, London, 102–121.

T. McGee and P. Ericsson. 2002. The Politics of the Program: MS Word as the Invisible Grammarian, *Computers and Composition*, 19:453–470.

J. Milton. 2001. *Elements of a Written Interlanguage: a computational and corpus-based study of institutional influences on the acquisition of English by Hong Kong Chinese students*. HKUST, Hong Kong.

J. Milton. 2006. Resource-Rich Web-Based Feedback: helping learners become independent writers, In Hyland, K. and Hyland F. (eds.) *Feedback in Second Language Writing: Contexts and Issues*, Cambridge University Press, 123–137.

M. C. Pennington. 1992. Beyond off-the-shelf computer remedies for student writers: Alternatives to canned feedback. *System*, 20(4):423–447.

D. Schneider. and K. F. McCoy. 1998. Recognizing syntactic errors in the writing of second language learners. *Proceedings of the 36th conference on Association for Computational Linguistics* volume 2. Montreal, Quebec, Canada.

M. Trahey. and L. White. 1993. Positive evidence and preemption in the L2 classroom. *Studies in Second Language Acquisition*, 15:181–204.

J. Truscott. 1996. The case against grammar correction in L2 writing classes. *Language Learning*, 46(2): 327-369.

A. Vernon. 2000. Computerized grammar checkers 2000: capabilities, limitations, and pedagogical possibilities. *Computers and Composition*, 17:329–349.

B. Wampler. 2002. A computer scientist's lament: grammar has lost its technological edge. *The New York Times*.

H. A. Witkin, C. Moore, D. Goodenough, and P. Cox. 1977. Field Dependent and Field Independent Cognitive Styles and their Educational Implications, *Review of Educational Research*, 47:1–64.

X. Yi, J. Gao and W. B. Dolan. 2008. A Web-based English Proofing System for English as a Second Language Users *Proceedings of the Third International Joint Conference on Natural Language Processing* volume 1.

Learning Simple Wikipedia: A Cogitation in Ascertaining Abecedarian Language

Courtney Napoles and **Mark Dredze**
Center for Language and Speech Processing
Human Language Technology Center of Excellence
Johns Hopkins University
Baltimore, MD 21211
courtneyn@jhu.edu, mdredze@cs.jhu.edu

Abstract

Text simplification is the process of changing vocabulary and grammatical structure to create a more accessible version of the text while maintaining the underlying information and content. Automated tools for text simplification are a practical way to make large corpora of text accessible to a wider audience lacking high levels of fluency in the corpus language. In this work, we investigate the potential of Simple Wikipedia to assist automatic text simplification by building a statistical classification system that discriminates *simple* English from *ordinary* English. Most text simplification systems are based on hand-written rules (e.g., PEST (Carroll et al., 1999) and its module SYSTAR (Canning et al., 2000)), and therefore face limitations scaling and transferring across domains. The potential for using Simple Wikipedia for text simplification is significant; it contains nearly 60,000 articles with revision histories and aligned articles to ordinary English Wikipedia. Using articles from Simple Wikipedia and ordinary Wikipedia, we evaluated different classifiers and feature sets to identify the most discriminative features of simple English for use across domains. These findings help further understanding of what makes text simple and can be applied as a tool to help writers craft simple text.

1 Introduction

The availability of large collections of electronic texts is a boon to information seekers, however, advanced texts often require fluency in the language. Text simplification (TS) is an emerging area of text-to-text generation that focuses on increasing the readability of a given text. Potential applications can increase the accessibility of text, which has great value in education, public health, and safety, and can aid natural language processing tasks such as machine translation and text generation.

Corresponding to these applications, TS can be broken down into two rough categories depending on the target "reader." The first type of TS aims to increase human readability for people lacking high-level language skills, either because of age, education level, unfamiliarity with the language, or disability. Historically, generating this text has been done by hand, which is time consuming and expensive, especially when dealing with material that requires expertise, such as legal documents. Most current automatic TS systems rely on handwritten rules, e.g., PEST (Carroll et al., 1999), its SYSTAR module (Canning et al., 2000), and the method described by Siddharthan (2006). Systems using handwritten rules can be susceptible to changes in domains and need to be modified for each new domain or language. There has been some research into automatically learning the rules for simplifying text using aligned corpora (Daelemans et al., 2004; Yatskar et al., 2010), but these have yet to match the performance hand-crafted rule systems. An example of a manually simplified sentence can be found in table 1.

The second type of TS has the goal of increasing the machine readability of text to aid tasks such as information extraction, machine translation, generative summarization, and other text generation

Proceedings of the NAACL HLT 2010 Workshop on Computational Linguistics and Writing, pages 42–50,
Los Angeles, California, June 2010.

tasks for selecting and evaluating the best candidate output text. In machine translation, the evaluation tool most commonly used for evaluating output, the BLEU score (Papineni et al., 2001), rates the "goodness" of output based on n-gram overlap with human-generated text. However this metric has been criticized for not accurately measuring the fluency of text and there is active research into other metrics (Callison-Burch et al., 2006; Ye et al., 2007). Previous studies suggest that text simplified for machine and human comprehension are categorically different (Chae and Nenkova, 2009). Our research considers text simplified for human readers, but the findings can be used to identify features that discriminate simple text for both applications.

The process of TS can be divided into three aspects: removing extraneous or superfluous text, substituting more complex lexical and syntactic forms, and inserting information to offer further clarification where needed (Aluísio et al., 2008). In this regard, TS is related to several different natural language processing tasks such as text summarization, compression, machine translation, and paraphrasing.

While none of these tasks alone directly provide a solution to text simplification, techniques can be drawn from each. Summarization techniques can be used to identify the crucial, most informative parts of a text and compression can be used to remove superfluous words and phrases. In fact, in the Wikipedia documents analyzed for this research, the average length of a "simple" document is only 21% the length of an "ordinary" English document (although this may be an unintentional byproduct of how articles were simplified, as discussed in section 6.1).

In this paper we study the properties of language that differentiate simple from ordinary text for human readers. Specifically, we use statistical learning techniques to identify the most discriminative features of simple English and "ordinary" English using articles from Simple Wikipedia and English Wikipedia. We use cognitively motivated features as well as statistical measurements of a document's lexical, syntactic, and surface features. Our study demonstrates the validity and potential benefits of using Simple Wikipedia as a resource for TS research.

Ordinary text
Every person has the right to a name, in which is included a first name and surname. ... The alias chosen for legal activities has the same protection as given to the name.
Same text in simple language
Every person has the right to have a name, and the law protects people's names. Also, the law protects a person's alias. ... The name is made up of a first name and a surname (name = first name + surname).

Table 1: A text in ordinary and simple language from Aluísio et al. (2008).

2 Wikipedia as a Corpus

Wikipedia is a unique resource for natural language processing tasks due to its sheer size, accessibility, language diversity, article structure, inter-document links, and inter-language document alignments. Denoyer and Gallinari (2006) introduced the Wikipedia XML Corpus, with 1.5 million documents in eight languages from Wikipedia, that stored the rich structural information of Wikipedia with XML. This corpus was designed specifically for XML retrieval but has uses in natural language processing, categorization, machine translation, entity ranking, etc. YAWN (Schenkel et al., 2007), a Wikipedia XML corpus with semantic tags, is another example of exploiting Wikipedia's structural information. Wikipedia provides XML site dumps every few weeks in all languages as well as static HTML dumps.

A diverse array of NLP research in the past few years has used Wikipedia, such as for word sense disambiguation (Mihalcea, 2007), classification (Gantner and Schmidt-Thieme, 2009), machine translation (Smith et al., 2010), coreference resolution (Versley et al., 2008; Yang and Su, 2007), sentence extraction for summarization (Biadsy et al., 2008), information retrieval (Müller and Gurevych, 2008), and semantic role labeling (Ponzetto and Strube, 2006), to name a few. However, except for very recent work by Yatskar et al. (2010), to our knowledge there has not been comparable research in using Wikipedia for text simplification.

Ordinary Wikipedia
Hawking was the Lucasian Professor of Mathematics at the University of Cambridge for thirty years, taking up the post in 1979 and retiring on 1 October 2009.
Simple Wikipedia
Hawking was a professor of mathematics at the University of Cambridge (a position that Isaac Newton once had). He retired on October 1st 2009.

Table 2: Comparable sentences from the ordinary Wikipedia and Simple Wikipedia entry for "Stephen Hawking."

Coarse Tag	Penn Treebank Tags
DET	DT, PDT
ADJ	JJ, JJR, JJS
N	NN, NNS, NP, NPS, PRP, FW
ADV	RB, RBR, RBS
V	VB, VBN, VBG, VBP, VBZ, MD
WH	WDT, WP, WP$, WRB

Table 3: A mapping of the Penn Treebank tags to a coarse tagset used to generate features.

What makes Wikipedia an excellent resource for text simplification is the new Simple Wikipedia project[1], a collection of 58,000 English Wikipedia articles that have been rewritten in Simple English, which uses basic vocabulary and less complex grammar to make the content of Wikipedia accessible to students, children, adults with learning difficulties, and non-native English speakers. In addition to being a large corpus, these articles are linked to their ordinary Wikipedia counterparts, so for each article both a simple and an ordinary version are available. Furthermore, on inspection many articles in Simple Wikipedia appear to be copied and edited from the corresponding ordinary Wikipedia article. This information, together with revision history and flags signifying unsimplified text, can provide a scale of information on the text-simplification process previously unavailable. Example sentences from Simple Wikipedia and ordinary Wikipedia are shown in table 2.

We used articles from Simple Wikipedia and ordinary English Wikipedia to create a large corpus of simple and ordinary articles for our experiments. In order to experiment with models that work across domains, the corpus includes articles from nine of the primary categories identified in Simple Wikipedia: Everyday Life, Geography, History, Knowledge, Literature, Media, People, Religion, and Science. A total of 55,433 ordinary and 42,973 simple articles were extracted and processed from English Wikipedia and Simple Wikipedia, respectively. Each document contains at least two sentences. Additionally, the corpus contains only the main text body of each article and does not consider info boxes, tables, lists, external and cross-references, and other structural features. The experiments that follow randomly extract documents and sentences from this collection.

Before extracting features, we ran a series of natural language processing tools to preprocess the collection. First, all of the XML and "wiki markup" was removed. Each document was split into sentences using the Punkt sentence tokenizer (Kiss and Strunk, 2006) in NLTK (Bird and Loper, 2004). We then parsed each sentence using the PCFG parser of Huang and Harper (2009), a modified version of the Berkeley parser (Petrov et al., 2006; Petrov and Klein, 2007), for the tree structure and part-of-speech tags.

3 Task Setup

To evaluate the feasibility of learning simple and ordinary texts, we sought to identify text properties that differentiated between these classes. Using the two document collections, we constructed a simple binary classification task: label a piece of text as either simple or ordinary. The text was labeled according to its source: simple or ordinary Wikipedia. From each piece of text, we extracted a set of features designed to capture differences between the texts, using cognitively motivated features based on a document's lexical, syntactic, and surface features. We first describe our features and then our experimental setup.

[1] `http://simple.wikipedia.org/`

4 Features

We began by examining the guidelines for writing Simple Wikipedia pages.[2] These guidelines suggest that articles use only the 1000 most common and basic English words and contain simple grammar and short sentences. Articles should be short but can be longer if they need to explain vocabulary words necessary to understand the topic. Additionally, words should appear on lists of basic English words, such as the Voice of America Special English words list (Voice Of America, 2009) or the Ogden Basic English list (Ogden, 1930). Idioms should be avoided as well as compounds and the passive voice as opposed to a single simple verb.

To capture these properties in the text, we created four classes of features: lexical, part-of-speech, surface, and parse. Several of our features have previously been used for measuring text fluency (Aluísio et al., 2008; Chae and Nenkova, 2009; Feng et al., 2009; Petersen and Ostendorf, 2007).

Lexical. Previous work by Feng et al. (2009) suggests that the document vocabulary is a good predictor of document readability. Simple texts are more likely to use basic words more often as opposed to more complicated, domain-specific words used in ordinary texts. To capture these features we used a unigram bag-of-words representation. We note that lexical features are unlikely to be useful unless we have access to a large training corpus that allowed the estimation of the relative frequency of words (Chae and Nenkova, 2009). Additionally, we can expect lexical features to be very fragile for cross-domain experiments as they are especially susceptible to changes in domain vocabulary. Nevertheless, we include these features as a baseline in our experiments.

Parts of speech. A clear focus of the simple text guidelines is grammar and word type. One way of representing this information is by measuring the relative frequency of different types of parts of speech. We consider simple unigram part-of-speech tag information. We measured the normalized counts and relative frequency of part-of-speech tags and counts of bigram part-of-speech tags in each piece of text. Since Devlin and Unthank (2006) has shown that word order (subject verb object (SVO), object verb subject (OVS), etc.) is correlated with readability, we also included a reduced tagset to capture grammatical patterns (table 3). We also included normalized counts of these reduced tags in the model.

Feature	Simple	Ordinary
Tokens	158	4332
Types	100	1446
Sentences	10	172
Average sentence length	15.80	25.19
Type-token ratio	0.63	0.33
Percent simple words	0.31	0.08
Not BE850 type-token ratio	0.65	0.30
BE850 type-token ratio	0.59	0.67

Table 4: A comparison of the article "Stephen Hawking" from Simple and ordinary Wikipedia.

Surface features. While lexical items may be important, more general properties can be extracted from the lexical forms. We can also include features that correspond to surface information in the text. These features include document length, sentence length, word length, numbers of lexical types and tokens, and the ratio of types to tokens. All words are labeled as basic or not basic according to Ogden's Basic English 850 (BE850) list (Ogden, 1930).[3] In order to measure the lexical complexity of a document, we include features for the number of BE850 words, the ratio of BE850 words to total words, and the type-token ratio of BE850 and non-BE850 words. Investigating the frequency and productivity of words not in the BE850 list will hopefully improve the flexibility of our model to work across domains and not learn any particular jargon. We also hope that the relative frequency and productivity measures of simple and non-simple words will codify the lexical choices of a sentence while avoiding the aforementioned problems with including specific lexical items.

[2] `http://simple.wikipedia.org/wiki/Wikipedia:Simple_English_Wikipedia`

[3] Wikipedia advocates using words that appear on the BE850 list. Ogden also provides extended Basic English vocabulary lists, totaling 2000 Basic English words, but these words tend to be more specialized or domain specific. For the purposes of this study only words in BE850 were used.

Table 4 shows the difference in some surface statistics in an aligned document from Simple and ordinary Wikipedia. In this example, nearly one-third of the words in the simple document are from the BE850 while less than a tenth of the words in the ordinary document are. Additionally, the productivity of words, particularly non-BE850 words, is much higher in the ordinary document. There are also clear differences in the length of the documents, and on average documents from ordinary Wikipedia are more than four times longer than documents from Simple Wikipedia.

Syntactic parse. As previously mentioned, a number of Wikipedia's writing guidelines focus on general grammatical rules of sentence structure. Evidence of these rules may be captured in the syntactic parse of the sentences in the text. Chae and Nenkova (2009) studied text fluency in the context of machine translation and found strong correlations between parse tree structures and sentence fluency.

In order to represent the structural complexity of the text, we collected extracted features from the parse trees. Our features included the frequency and length of noun phrases, verb phrases, prepositional phrases, and relative clauses (including embedded structures). We also considered relative ratios, such as the ratio of noun to verb phrases, prepositional to noun phrases, and relative clauses to noun phrases. We used the length of the longest noun phrase as a signal of complexity, and we also sought features that measured how typical the sentences were of English text. We included some of the features from the parser reranking work of Charniak and Johnson (2005): the height of the parse tree and the number of right branches from the root of the tree to the furthest right leaf that is not punctuation.

5 Experiments

Using the feature sets described above, we evaluated a simple/ordinary text classifier in several settings on each category. First, we considered the task of document classification, where a classifier determines whether a full Wikipedia article was from ordinary English Wikipedia or Simple Wikipedia. For each category of articles, we measured accuracy on this binary classification task using 10-fold cross-validation. In the second setting, we considered the performance of a sentence-level classifier. The classifier labeled each sentence as either ordinary or simple and we report results using 10-fold cross-validation on a random split of the sentences. For both settings we also evaluated a single classifier trained on all categories.

We next considered cross-category performance: how would a classifier trained to detect differences between simple and ordinary examples from one category do when tested on another category. In this experiment, we trained a single classifier on data from a single category and used the classifier to label examples from each of the other categories. We report the accuracy on each category in these transfer experiments.

For learning we require a binary classifier training algorithm. We evaluated several learning algorithms for classification and report results for each one: a) MIRA—a large margin online learning algorithm (Crammer et al., 2006). Online learning algorithms observe examples sequentially and up-

Category	**Documents**	**Sentences**
Everyday Life	15,124	7,392
Geography	10,470	5,852
History	5,174	1,644
Literature	992	438
Media	502	429
People	4,326	1,562
Religion	1,863	1,581
Science	25,787	21,054
All	64,238	39,952

Table 5: The number of examples available in each category. To compare experiments in each category we used at most 2000 instances in each experiment.

Feature class		**Features**
Lexical		**522,153**
Part of speech		**2478**
	tags	45
	tag pairs	1972
	tags (reduced)	22
	tag pairs (reduced)	484
Parse		**11**
Surface		**9**

Table 6: The number of features in each feature class.

date the current hypothesis after each observation; b) Confidence Weighted (CW) learning—a probabilistic large margin online learning algorithm (Dredze et al., 2008); c) Maximum Entropy—a log-linear discriminative classifier (Berger et al., 1996); and d) Support Vector Machines (SVM)—a large margin discriminator (Joachims, 1998).

For each experiment, we used default settings of the parameters and 10 online iterations for the online methods (MIRA, CW). To create a fair comparison for each category, we limited the number of examples to a maximum of 2000.

6 Results

For the first task of document classification, we saw at least 90% mean accuracy with each of the classifiers. Using all features, SVM and Maximum Entropy performed almost perfectly. The online classifiers, CW and MIRA, displayed similar preference to the larger feature sets, lexical and part-of-speech counts. When using just lexical counts, both CW and MIRA were more accurate than the SVM and Maximum Entropy (reporting 92.95% and 86.55% versus 75.00% and 78.75%, respectively). For all classifiers, the models using the counts of part-of-speech tags did better than classifiers trained on the surface features and on the parse features. This is surprising, since we expected the surface features to be robust predictors of the document class, mainly because the average ordinary Wikipedia article in our corpus is about four times longer than the average Simple Wikipedia article. We also expected the syntactic features to be a strong predictor of the document class since more complicated parse trees correspond to more complex sentences.

For each classifier, we looked at its performance without its less predictive feature categories, and for CW the inclusion of the surface features decreased performance noticeably. The best CW classifiers used either part-of-speech and lexical features (95.95%) or just part-of-speech features (95.80%). The parse features, which by themselves only yielded 64.60% accuracy, when combined with part-of-speech and lexical features showed high accuracy as well (95.60%). MIRA also showed higher accuracy when surface features were not included (from 97.50% mean accuracy with all features to 97.75% with all but surface features).

The best SVM classifier used all four feature classes, but had nearly as good accuracy with just part-of-speech counts and surface features (99.85% mean accuracy) and with surface and parse features (also 99.85% accuracy). Maximum Entropy, on the other hand, improved slightly when the lexical and parse features were not included (from 99.45% mean accuracy with all feature classes to 99.55%).

We examined the weights learned by the classifiers to determine the features that were effective for learning. We selected the features with the highest absolute weight for a MIRA classifier trained on all categories. The most predictive features for document classification were the sentence length (shorter favors Simple), the length of the longest NP (longer favors ordinary), the number of sentences (more favors ordinary), the average number of prepositional phrases and noun phrases per sentence, the height of the parse tree, and the number of adjectives. The most predictive features for sentence classification were the ratio of different tree non-terminals (VP, S, NP, S-Bar) to the number of words in the sentence, the ratio of the total height of the productions in a tree to the height of the tree, and the extent to which the tree was right branching. These features are consistent with the rules described above for simple text.

Next we looked at a pairwise comparison of how the classifiers perform when trained on one category and tested on another. Surprisingly, the results were robust across categories, across classifiers. Using the best feature class as determined in the first task, the average drop in accuracy when trained on each domain was very low across all classifiers (the mean accuracy rate of each cross-category classification was at least 90%). Table 6 shows the mean change in accuracy from CW models trained and tested on the same category to the models trained and tested on different categories. When trained on the Everyday Life category, the model actually showed a mean increase in accuracy when predicting other categories.

In the final task, we trained binary classifiers to identify simple sentences in isolation. The mean accuracy was lower for this task than for the document classification task, and we anticipated individual sentences to be more difficult to classify because each sentence only carries a fraction of the

Classifier	All features	Lexical	POS	Surface	Parse
CW	86.40%	92.95%	**95.80%**	69.80%	64.60%
MIRA	**97.50%**	86.55%	94.55%	79.65%	66.90%
MaxEnt	**99.45%**	78.75%	96.25%	86.90%	80.70%
SVM	**99.90%**	75.00%	96.60%	89.75%	82.70%

Table 7: Mean accuracy of all classifiers on the document classification task.

Classifier	All features	POS	Surface	Parse
CW	73.20%	**74.45%**	57.40%	62.25%
MIRA	71.15%	**72.65%**	56.50%	56.45%
MaxEnt	**80.80%**	77.65%	71.30%	69.00%
SVM	**77.00%**	76.40%	72.55%	73.00%

Table 8: Mean accuracy of all classifiers on the sentence classification task.

Category	Mean accuracy change
Everyday life	+1.42%
Geography	−4.29%
History	−1.01%
Literature	−1.84%
Media	−0.56%
People	−0.20%
Religion	−0.56%
Science	−2.50%

Table 9: Mean accuracy drop for a CW model trained on one category and tested on all other categories. Negative numbers indicate a decrease in performance.

information held in an entire document. It is common to have short, simple sentences as part of ordinary English text, although they will not make up the whole. However results were still promising, with between 72% and 80% mean accuracy. With CW and MIRA, the classifiers benefited from training on all categories, while MaxEnt and SVM in-category and all-category models achieved similar accuracy levels, but the results on cross-category tests were more variable than in the document classification. There was also no consistency across features and classifiers with regard to category-to-category classification. Overall the results of the sentence classification task are encouraging and show promise for detecting individual simple sentences taken out of context.

6.1 Discussion

The classifiers performed robustly for the document-level classification task, although the corpus itself may have biased the model due to the longer average length of ordinary documents, which we tried to address by filtering out articles with only one or two sentences. Cursory inspection suggests that there is overlap between many Simple Wikipedia articles and their corresponding ordinary English articles, since a large number of Simple Wikipedia documents appear to be generated directly from the English Wikipedia articles with more complicated subsections of the documents omitted from the Simple article.

The sentence classification task could be improved by better labeling of sentences. In these experiments, we assumed that every sentence in an ordinary document would be ordinary (i.e., not simple) and vice versa for simple documents. However it is not the case that ordinary English text contains only complicated sentences. In future research we can use human annotated sentences for building the classifiers. The features we used in this research suggest that simple text is created from categorical lexical and syntactic replacement, but more complicated, technical, or detailed oriented text may require more rewriting, and would be of more interest in future research.

7 Conclusion and Future Work

We have demonstrated the ability to automatically identify texts as either simple or ordinary at both the document and sentence levels using a variety of features based on the word usage and grammatical structures in text. Our statistical analysis has identified relevant features for this task accessible to computational systems. Immediate applications of the classifiers created in this research for text simplification include editing tools that can identify parts of a text that may be difficult to understand or for word processors, in order to notify writers of complicated sentences in real time.

Using this initial exploration of Simple Wikipedia, we plan to continue working in a number of directions. First, we will explore additional robust indications of text difficulty. For example, Aluísio et al. (2008) claim that sentences that are easier to read are also easier to parse, so the entropy of the parser or confidence in the output may be indicative of a text's difficulty. Additionally, language models trained on large corpora can assign probability scores to texts, which may indicate text difficulty. Of particular interest are syntactic language models that incorporate some of the syntactic observations in this paper (Filimonov and Harper, 2009).

Our next goal will be to look at parallel sentences to learn rules for simplifying text. One of the advantages of the Wikipedia collection is the parallel articles in ordinary English Wikipedia and Simple Wikipedia. While the content of the articles can differ, these are excellent examples of comparable texts that can be useful for learning simplification rules. Such learning can draw from machine translation, which learns rules that translate between languages. The related task of paraphrase extraction could also provide comparable phrases, one of which can be identified as a simplified version of the other (Bannard and Callison-Burch, 2005). An additional resource available in Simple Wikipedia is the flagging of articles as not simple. By examining the revision history of articles whose flags have been changed, we can discover changes that simplified texts. Initial work on this topic has automatically learned which edits correspond to text simplifications (Yatskar et al., 2010).

Text simplification may necessitate the removal of whole phrases, sentences, or even paragraphs, as, according to the writing guidelines for Wikipedia Simple (Wikipedia, 2009), the articles should not exceed a specified length, and some concepts may not be explainable using the lexicon of Basic English. In some situations, adding new text to explain confusing but crucial points may serve to aid the reader, and text generation needs to be further investigated to make text simplification an automatic process.

Acknowledgements

The authors would like to thank Mary Harper for her help in parsing our corpus.

References

S.M. Aluísio, L. Specia, T.A.S. Pardo, E.G. Maziero, and R.P.M. Fortes. 2008. Brazilian portuguese automatic text simplification systems. In *DocEng*.

Colin Bannard and Chris Callison-Burch. 2005. Paraphrasing with bilingual parallel corpora. In *Association for Computational Linguistics (ACL)*.

A.L. Berger, V.J.D. Pietra, and S.A.D. Pietra. 1996. A maximum entropy approach to natural language processing. *Computational linguistics*, 22(1):39–71.

F. Biadsy, J. Hirschberg, E. Filatova, and LLC InforSense. 2008. An unsupervised approach to biography production using Wikipedia. In *Association for Computational Linguistics (ACL)*.

S. Bird and E. Loper. 2004. NLTK: The natural language toolkit. *Proceedings of the ACL demonstration session*, pages 214–217.

C. Callison-Burch, M. Osborne, and P. Koehn. 2006. Re-evaluating the role of BLEU in machine translation research. In *European Conference for Computational Linguistics (EACL)*, volume 2006, pages 249–256.

Y. Canning, J. Tait, J. Archibald, and R. Crawley. 2000. Cohesive generation of syntactically simplified newspaper text. *Lecture notes in computer science*, pages 145–150.

J. Carroll, G. Minnen, D. Pearce, Y. Canning, S. Devlin, and J. Tait. 1999. Simplifying text for language-impaired readers. In *European Conference for Computational Linguistics (EACL)*, pages 269–270.

J. Chae and A. Nenkova. 2009. Predicting the fluency of text with shallow structural features. In *European Conference for Computational Linguistics (EACL)*, pages 139–147.

E. Charniak and M. Johnson. 2005. Coarse-to-fine n-best parsing and MaxEnt discriminative reranking. In *Association for Computational Linguistics (ACL)*, page 180. Association for Computational Linguistics.

Koby Crammer, Ofer Dekel, Joseph Keshet, Shai Shalev-Shwartz, and Yoram Singer. 2006. Online passive-aggressive algorithms. *Journal of Machine Learning Research (JMLR)*.

W. Daelemans, A. Höthker, and E Tjong Kim Sang. 2004. Automatic sentence simplification for subtitling in Dutch and English. In *Conference on Language Resources and Evaluation (LREC)*, pages 1045–1048.

Ludovic Denoyer and Patrick Gallinari. 2006. The Wikipedia XML Corpus. *SIGIR Forum*.

S. Devlin and G. Unthank. 2006. Helping aphasic people process online information. In *SIGACCESS Conference on Computers and Accessibility*.

Mark Dredze, Koby Crammer, and Fernando Pereira. 2008. Confidence-weighted linear classification. In *International Conference on Machine Learning (ICML)*.

L. Feng, N. Elhadad, and M. Huenerfauth. 2009. Cognitively motivated features for readability assessment. In *European Conference for Computational Linguistics (EACL)*.

Denis Filimonov and Mary Harper. 2009. A joint language model with fine-grain syntactic tags. In *Empirical Methods in Natural Language Processing (EMNLP)*.

Z. Gantner and L. Schmidt-Thieme. 2009. Automatic content-based categorization of Wikipedia articles. In *Association for Computational Linguistics (ACL)*.

Z. Huang and M. Harper. 2009. Self-training pcfg grammars with latent annotations across languages. In *Empirical Methods in Natural Language Processing (EMNLP)*.

T. Joachims. 1998. Text categorization with support vector machines: Learning with many relevant features. In *European Conference on Machine Learning (ECML)*.

T. Kiss and J. Strunk. 2006. Unsupervised multilingual sentence boundary detection. *Computational Linguistics*, 32(4):485–525.

R. Mihalcea. 2007. Using Wikipedia for automatic word sense disambiguation. In *North American Chapter of the Association for Computational Linguistics (NAACL)*.

C. Müller and I. Gurevych. 2008. Using Wikipedia and Wiktionary in domain-specific information retrieval. In *Working Notes of the Annual CLEF Meeting*. Springer.

C.K. Ogden. 1930. *Basic English: A General Introduction with Rules and Grammar*. Paul Treber & Co., Ltd.

K. Papineni, S. Roukos, T. Ward, and W.J. Zhu. 2001. BLEU: a method for automatic evaluation of machine translation. In *Association for Computational Linguistics (ACL)*.

S.E. Petersen and M. Ostendorf. 2007. Text simplification for language learners: A corpus analysis. In *The Speech and Language Technology for Education Workshop*, pages 69–72.

Slav Petrov and Dan Klein. 2007. Improved inference for unlexicalized parsing. In *North American Chapter of the Association for Computational Linguistics (NAACL)*.

Slav Petrov, Leon Barrett, Romain Thibaux, and Dan Klein. 2006. Learning accurate, compact, and interpretable tree annotation. In *Association for Computational Linguistics (ACL)*.

S.P. Ponzetto and M. Strube. 2006. Exploiting semantic role labeling, WordNet and Wikipedia for coreference resolution. In *North American Chapter of the Association for Computational Linguistics (NAACL)*.

R. Schenkel, F. Suchanek, and G. Kasneci. 2007. YAWN: A semantically annotated Wikipedia XML corpus. In *Proceedings of GI-Fachtagung für Datenbanksysteme in Business, Technologie und Web (BTW2007)*.

A. Siddharthan. 2006. Syntactic simplification and text cohesion. *Research on Language & Computation*, 4(1):77–109.

Jason Smith, Chris Quirk, and Kristina Toutanova. 2010. Extracting parallel sentences from comparable corpora using document level alignment. In *North American Chapter of the Association for Computational Linguistics (NAACL)*.

Y. Versley, S.P. Ponzetto, M. Poesio, V. Eidelman, A. Jern, J. Smith, X. Yang, and A. Moschitti. 2008. BART: A modular toolkit for coreference resolution. In *Association for Computational Linguistics (ACL) Demo Session*.

Voice Of America. 2009. Word book, 2009 edition. www.voaspecialenglish.com, February.

Wikipedia. 2009. Simple Wikipedia English. http://en.wikipedia.org/wiki/Citing_Wikipedia, October.

X. Yang and J. Su. 2007. Coreference resolution using semantic relatedness information from automatically discovered patterns. In *Association for Computational Linguistics (ACL)*.

Mark Yatskar, Bo Pang, Cristian Danescu-Niculescu-Mizil, and Lillian Lee. 2010. For the sake of simplicity: Experiments with unsupervised extraction of lexical simplifications. In *North American Chapter of the Association for Computational Linguistics (NAACL)*.

Y. Ye, M. Zhou, and C.Y. Lin. 2007. Sentence level machine translation evaluation as a ranking problem: one step aside from BLEU. In *ACL Workshop on statistical machine translation*.

Questions Worth Asking: Intersections between Writing Research and Computational Linguistics

Anne Ruggles Gere and **Laura Aull**
University of Michigan
Ann Arbor, MI 48104, USA

Abstract

Rather than explain research that has already been carried out, this paper describes a specific context of writing instruction and poses questions about how research on writing and computational linguistics might be brought together to address three pressing issues: the validity of Directed Self-Placement; the relationship between confidence and competence in student writing; and strategies to help English Language Learners, especially those in the category of Generation 1.5, improve their writing.

1 Introduction

In this paper we would like to explore questions that hover at the intersection of writing research and computational linguistics. First, however, we would like to explain the context of our work since we believe that context is a shaping force in any research on writing. The site where we work is the Sweetland Center for Writing at the University of Michigan, and this Center is responsible for the placement of some 4000 first-year students in several different colleges including LSA, Nursing, Kinesiology, Art and Design, and Music.

The majority of students who enroll at this university have performed well on tests and in high school. Only approximately 5% have a high school GPA under 3.3 or a SAT verbal below 530. The university also enrolls a significant (approximately 5%) number of international students who are English Language Learners, along with an unknown number of Generation 1.5 students who are also learning to manage various aspects of academic English but who are very difficult to identify because they do not have the clear markers of international students. The Center is also responsible for oversight of all courses that meet the First Year Writing Requirement and the Upper Level Writing Requirement.

First-year students enroll in either a developmental course, Writing 100, or one of the seven different courses that satisfy the First Year Writing Requirement (FYW). For nearly a decade students decided between the two, in concert with their advisors, by participating in a form of Directed Self-Placement (DSP).

DSP, which came into use in the United States during the final years of the 20th century, puts into student hands the decision about placement in writing courses. DSP was first implemented at colleges small enough to provide significant amounts of one-on-one time between students and advisors and/or writing instructors. DSP has taken various forms, depending upon the local context, but it always asks students to assess their own abilities as writers.

In the version of DSP first implemented at our university, students answered seven questions about their reading habits and their writing practices, along with their grades and test scores. The questions used from 2000 to 2005 gave more attention to mastery, as in "I have learned the correct forms of standard written English and make few mistakes in sentence construction,

Proceedings of the NAACL HLT 2010 Workshop on Computational Linguistics and Writing, pages 51–55,
Los Angeles, California, June 2010.

punctuation, and usage," while the survey used from 2006 to 2008 focused more on comfort or confidence, as in "I am comfortable using standard written English, including the correct forms of grammar, punctuation, and sentence construction."

Significantly, the number of students who received a recommendation for Writing Practicum dropped dramatically—from approximately 1000 to approximately 200—when the second form of the survey was introduced. The decisions about enrollment, of course, remained in the hands of students, and it is worth noting that the percentage of students who followed the recommendation generated by the survey increased from 15% to 35%.

2 Questions of Validity

Analysis of the DSP process that had been in place from 2000 to 2008 (under both sets of questions) showed that it had little validity (Gere et al., forthcoming). It lacked substantive validity because of the time gap between completion of the survey and course selection; it lacked structural validity because the survey questions bore little relation to the construct of writing central in the FYW courses; it lacked validity of generalizability because only a small percentage of students followed the recommendation generated by the DSP survey; it lacked external validity because there was a low correlation between students' scores on other measures and on the DSP survey; and it lacked consequential validity because the construct of writing operating in the Writing 100 course bore little relation to that emphasized in the DSP survey. This analysis, combined with the fact that students' perception of the importance of writing was influenced by the contrast between answering seven multiple choice questions and completing substantive tests in math, chemistry and foreign languages, led to a reconfiguring of the DSP process to include writing an essay and answering questions about that process as well as about literacy practices more generally.

Beginning in the fall of 2009, entering first-year students at our university write an evidence-based argument in response to a 3500 word publication. Essays of entering students are submitted electronically and are delivered to individual instructors of students' first writing class so that they become incorporated into instruction. The Writing 100 course has been redesigned so that it is aligned with the construct of writing in the DSP process and in the FYW course.

In other words, we now have a large and growing corpus of student writing, and it would be helpful to think through how we might make best use of it, with regard to questions of validity as well as other issues. The DSP essay corpus currently includes over 3500 student essays comprising over three million words, and by the end of August 2010, these numbers will double as a new cohort of students enters the University. All the texts in the initial corpus were written by incoming first-year students in response to a prompt for an evidence-based argument about a Malcom Gladwell essay that discusses the difficulty of predicting which candidates will become good teachers—or quarterbacks or financial advisors. Instructions included a recommendation to consider these features: focus or development around a clear central thesis or argument; structure or organization that elaborates on and supports the central argument; and evidence or well-chosen examples from the text to support claims.

In addition to this corpus, we have the potential to create a smaller corpus of student writing produced in first writing classes, both Writing 100 and courses that satisfy the First Year Writing Requirement, as well as personal narratives written as part of each student's admission portfolio. In coming years, we could also collect samples of writing across the entire undergraduate experience of a subset of students. One of the questions we would like to discuss, then, centers on what decisions we should make about structuring additional corpora so as to take best advantage of the texts and materials available to us.

One clear direction for our work is to continue the investigation of validity to determine the extent to which the modifications in the DSP process and in Writing 100 enhance the validity of the placement process now in place. In particular, it would be useful to learn more about the consequential validity of the DSP process since its main result or consequence is enrollment in either Writing 100 or a course that meets the First Year Writing Requirement. Among the possible questions to investigate are these:

- How can we best use the existing corpus and additional ones we might create to determine the extent to which the writing of students who elect Writing 100 differs from that of students who choose to enroll immediately in courses that meet the FYW requirement?
- How might we best create subgroups (and subcorpora) to understand how writers in each subgroup articulate arguments and use evidence?

The evidence-based argument is central in both contexts of first writing courses, and the construct of writing that operates in the DSP and in Writing 100 includes features of formal, purposeful, coherent, complex, audience-aware, and evidence-based writing. A variety of rhetorical choices in academic writing help writers achieve these features; for example, we know from the work of Hyland (2005) that effective writers use textual signals to pull readers along their line of argument, so one approach in our research would be to compare the writing of students who elect Writing 100 and those who do not in terms of their use of textual signs that make the terms of their arguments clear.

Given student data and surveys we have access to, we also have the capacity to create subcorpora based on student grades and scores, English nativeness, student high school types, or students' reported attributes such as confidence or writing experience. Understanding how writers in various subgroups construct arguments will help answer key questions about the validity of the current form of DSP, and we welcome discussion of how quantitative linguistics can aid in that process.

3 Questions of Confidence

Another set of questions emerges from analysis of students' responses to the DSP survey. This examination showed that there were a few "trigger" questions that influenced students' choices about which writing course to take. That is, certain questions were the ones that propelled the greatest number of students to take or not take Writing 100. Most prominent among these were the questions dealing with the issue of confidence, as in "I am confident about my ability to comprehend unfamiliar texts."

In a subsequent survey of students who had already enrolled in either Writing 100 or a course that meets the FYW requirement, the issue of confidence became even more prominent. When asked to rank the importance of various factors in their self-placement in a writing course, "confidence in my own writing ability" was the number one factor for the great majority of students.

The next most important factor, input from an academic advisor, received less than half as many "most important" responses. This finding is significant in at least two ways, and it also raises questions that can call upon the resources of computational linguistics. One dimension of the significance of the confidence issue is that confidence is central to the theory underlying Directed Self-Placement. The literature on DSP positions confidence as the goal of a developmental course and a desired result of a FYW course is that students will develop "writing confidence." Indeed some scholars have suggested that DSP may be more a measure of confidence than of writing ability (Reynolds, 2003). The importance of confidence is magnified by the fact that confidence is frequently equated with competence in writing; it is also credited with driving out apprehension about writing, and with enhancing the authorial identity of students.

Another significant dimension of confidence, however, troubles its relationship to DSP and to writing more generally because empirical studies show that confidence in writing does not have a fixed or stable meaning. The person who expresses considerable confidence in writing essays may experience and express a lack of confidence about writing in another genre or form such as a grant proposal or lab report. The student who is a confident writer in high school may have a significant loss of confidence when faced with the writing tasks of college or the workplace. Writers who express confidence may or may not be able to produce writing that is recognized by others as "good." And those confident writers who are recognized for "good" writing in one context may not be so recognized in other contests.

Confidence, which is closely allied with self-efficacy, is task specific, and this complicates the meaning of writing confidence. Given the importance and instability of confidence in relation to writing and to DSP specifically, it will be useful to learn more about how confidence is manifested in student writing. Because the research on the relationship between confidence and competence in writing is mixed, it will be important to explore this relationship more closely. The corpus of student writing along with information about the questions to which students respond, particularly those focused on confidence, allows us to compare patterns in subcorpora of writing done by students who self-identify as confident academic writers versus those who do not. These resources provide useful data for beginning to address a number of questions that emerge from the issue of confidence in DSP, and in writing more generally.

One way to understand more about the nature and function of confidence is to consider its relationship to competence in writing. Our preliminary investigation of the relationship between student confidence and competence has focused on features that research shows to correlate with highly ranked writing. Two features emerge directly from the genre of writing required by the DSP prompt. One is organization, and we can learn something about this from analyzing the corpus for discourse markers such as transition words, since such markers correlate highly with effective argumentative writing (Xing et al., 2008). Another is reference to the reading material because research (Woodward-Kron, 2003) shows the importance of interacting with multiple voices to make effective arguments, and examples from the text are one of the features mentioned in the DSP prompt.

In addition, there are features that correlate with effective writing more generally. One of these is text length because research shows that students who produce more words typically receive higher scores, particularly on timed writing tests (Friedlander, 1990). Another is type/token ratios because research shows that students who use a greater variety of words are typically identified as better writers (Engber, 1993).

We believe that analyzing the entire corpus as well as subgroups identified by levels of self-proclaimed confidence for features like transition words and references to the reading material as well as text length and type-token ratios will provide some insight into the relationship between confidence and competence in writing. At the same time, however, we welcome discussion on how we might nuance this investigation further by calling upon other resources of computational linguistics.

4 Questions of Language Learning

As mentioned earlier, one of the subgroups within the larger university population is English Language Learners. Briefly, international students at our university who score below a fixed threshold on the TESOL are required to take a second test, the AEE, in addition to participating in the DSP process. The survey questions to which they respond are slightly different from those answered by native speakers, and the essay they read includes glosses to explain culturally specific terms. This combination of accommodations and measures is relatively effective in identifying students who need special intervention in order to write well in English.

But, as current research shows, there is another population of English Language Learners that is much less visible than the typical international students—the population typically known as Generation 1.5. These students are much more fully assimilated into US culture, usually because they have lived in this country for an extended period and have attended US schools. However, their writing frequently manifests many of the same difficulties as the more easily identified English Language Learners. One of the chief instructional challenges posed by Generation 1.5 students is that they are not easy to identify, and their instructional needs are not clearly defined. Analysis of the DSP process at our university shows that Generation 1.5 students regularly fly under the radar of self-placement and find themselves struggling in writing classes. Anecdotal reports from instructors point to these students' difficulties, but we have no systematic way of identifying and helping them. This population, like that of ELL students, is currently growing each year, and it is becoming increasingly important to address its needs.

It is clear, however, that positioning English language learners and, especially, Generation 1.5 as deficient is not constructive. ELL and Generation 1.5 students are often constructed in highly positive terms such as hard-working and determined in high school and then positioned negatively as resistant and unmotivated when they enter college writing classes. The first challenge is to develop better ways of identifying Generation 1.5 students early in their university work so that they are not left to flounder, as they so often do, when they move into upper division courses. The double challenge of acquiring academic literacy while simultaneously acquiring proficiency in the English language frequently, as Short and Fitzsimmons (2007) show, becomes overwhelming to students who have many competencies and are highly motivated. The college writing class offers a space for equipping students who are learning English at the same time that they are leaning about college writing. In order for this to happen, however, we need to learn more about the specific nature of challenges faced by these students. Research by Wu (2007) shows that ability to adjust dialogic space is often difficult for L2 writers, and Hyland and Milton (1997) demonstrate that L2 writers frequently take a more authoritative and less nuanced stance, while more highly valued writing typically expresses more epistemic uncertainty.

As a first step, we will create a sub corpus of identified English Language Learners and use the rhetorical and interactive features of competence (organization, reference to reading, text length, lexical variety, and transition words) identified above to determine the extent to which these features identify levels of writing competence for this population. If we can isolate features that are characteristic of this population of English Language Learners, then we can attempt to apply the same features to the entire corpus in order to begin the process of identifying Generation 1.5 students.

We are less certain about how to use computational linguistics most effectively to identify ability to adjust dialogic space and take a more nuanced stance in writing. Nor, of course, are we certain that these features will be the most productive in helping us to identify Generation 1.5 students. Accordingly, we will welcome discussion of additional ways to use computational linguistics to identify Generation 1.5 students.

5 Conclusion

We have done some preliminary thinking and begun investigations of questions about validity, confidence and English Language Learners, and we welcome the opportunity to explore ways of uniting research in writing and in computational linguistics to further our investigation.

References

C. Engber. 1995. The relationship of lexical proficiency to the quality of ESL compositions. *Journal of Second Language Writing* 4(2):139–155.

A. Friedlander. 1990. Composing in English: Effects of a first language on writing in English as a second language In Barbara Kroll (Ed.) *Second Language Writing: Research Insights for the Classroom*, New York: Cambridge UP.

A. R. Gere, L. Aull, T. Green and A. Porter. (forthcoming). Assessing the validity of directed self-placement at a large university. *Assessing Writing.*

K. Hyland. 2005. Representing readers in writing: Student and expert practices. *Linguistics and Education* 16, 363–377.

K. Hyland, and J. Milton. 1997. Qualifications and certainty in L1 and L2 students writing. *Journal of Second Language Writing* 6(2):183–205.

E. J. Reynolds. 2003. The role of self-efficacy in writing and directed self-placement. In Daniel Royer and Roger Gilles (Eds.) *Directed Self-Placement: Principles and Practices*. Cresskill, NJ: Hampton Press, 73–104.

R. Woodward-Kron. 2003. Critical analysis and the journal article review assignment *Journal of English for Academic Purposes*, 6, 254–271.

M. Xing, J. Wang and K. Spencer. 2008. Raising Students' Awareness of cross-cultural contrastive rhetoric in English writing via an E-learning course. *Language Learning & Technology* 12(2):71–93.

Exploring Individual Differences in Student Writing with a Narrative Composition Support Environment

Julius Goth and **Alok Baikadi** and **Eun Ha** and **Jonathan Rowe** and **Bradford Mott** and **James Lester**

Department of Computer Science
North Carolina State University
Raleigh, NC, USA

{jgoth, abaikad, eha, jprowe, bwmott, lester}@ncsu.edu

Abstract

Novice writers face significant challenges as they learn to master the broad range of skills that contribute to composition. Novice and expert writers differ considerably, and devising effective composition support tools for novice writers requires a clear understanding of the process and products of writing. This paper reports on a study conducted with more than one hundred middle grade students interacting with a narrative composition support environment. The texts are found to pose important challenges for state-of-the-art natural language processing techniques. Furthermore, the study investigates the language usage of middle grade students, the cohesion and coherence of the resulting texts, and the relationship between students' language arts skills and their writing processes. The findings suggest that composition support environments require robust NLP tools that can account for the variations in students' writing in order to effectively support each phase of the writing process.

1 Introduction

Writing is fundamentally complex. Writers must simultaneously consider a constellation of factors during composition, including writing task requirements, knowledge of audience, domain knowledge, language usage, and tone (Hayes and Flower, 1981). Furthermore, effective writing involves sophisticated higher-order cognitive skills, such as synthesis of ideas, critical thinking, and self-regulation. Text genres, such as narrative or expository texts, also introduce distinct requirements and conventions (Hayes and Flower, 1981).

Because writing itself is complex, learning to write poses significant challenges for students. The central role of writing in communication, knowledge organization, and sensemaking points to the need to devise methods and tools with which writing skills can be effectively taught and learned (Graham, 2006). Intelligent tutoring systems (VanLehn, 2006) offer a promising means for delivering tailored writing support to students. However, developing intelligent tutors to scaffold student writing poses a number of technical and pedagogical hurdles. Texts written by novice writers are likely to exhibit significant variation in grammar, cohesion, coherence, and content quality; these characteristics are likely to be problematic for analysis by current natural language processing tools. Furthermore, students' individual differences in language arts skills, writing self-efficacy, domain knowledge, and motivation can have pedagogical implications. An effective intelligent writing tutor must do more than just parse and understand student texts; it must also provide tailored feedback that fosters effective writing processes and enhances student motivation for writing.

This paper explores several key questions for the design of intelligent composition support tools for novice writers. First, it investigates the performance of current syntactic parsing tools on a corpus of narrative texts written by middle grade students during interactions in a narrative composi-

Proceedings of the NAACL HLT 2010 Workshop on Computational Linguistics and Writing, pages 56–64,
Los Angeles, California, June 2010.

tion support environment. A *narrative composition support environment* aims to support the principal processes of writing, such as planning, revision, and text production. The second question the paper explores is how middle school students' language art skills affect the cohesion and coherence of texts produced during interactions with a narrative composition support environment. Third, the paper investigates how middle school students' language art skills affect their writing processes during interactions in a narrative composition support environment. Studying the interactions between the environment's support mechanisms and students' individual differences provides insights into the affordances and limitations of novices' writing abilities, as well as implications for the design of intelligent tutors for narrative writing.

The study presented here investigates novice writers' composition processes during interactions with a narrative composition support environment. In the study, 127 middle grade students interacted with the NARRATIVE THEATRE fable composition support environment. The NARRATIVE THEATRE uses a multimedia interface to guide students as they select key elements of their fable (e.g., moral, setting, characters), prompts students through an explicit, timed story planning process, and allows students to review their earlier planning decisions at any point during writing of the main text. Students' literacy ratings and log data from interactions with the NARRATIVE THEATRE environment are analyzed to investigate the differences between high- and low-skill students and their practice of key composition processes in the NARRATIVE THEATRE environment, including planning, text production, and revision. Coh-Metrix (Graesser et al., 2004) was also used to analyze the cohesion and coherence characteristics of the students' fables. The observations from this study offer important implications for the design of intelligent composition support tools for novice writers.

2 Related Work

Since Hayes and Flower first proposed their seminal model of writing nearly thirty years ago (1981), a rich body of work has investigated the cognitive functions supporting written composition. Foundational results are now in place on the core processes of writing, including idea generation (Galbraith et al., 2009), text production (Berninger et al., 2002), and revision (McCutchen et al., 1997). Furthermore, a detailed account of the composition process has begun to emerge across a range of writing experience levels (Graham et al., 2002) and text genres (Langer, 1985).

Particularly important for the design of composition support tools for novices is the emergence of a consensus account of the characteristics of novice writers' narrative composition processes. Empirical studies have suggested that notable differences exist between novice and expert writers, such as novices' use of knowledge-telling practices versus experts' use of knowledge-transformation practices during text production (Bereiter and Scardamalia, 1987). However, it has been argued that even novice writers can employ high-level knowledge-transformation processes when situated within an appropriate task environment with effective writing scaffolds (Cameron and Moshenko, 1996). Other work has found that students' domain and linguistic knowledge influences the coherence and quality of their expository writings (DeGroff, 1987). These findings underscore the importance of investigating methods for effective and engaging writing instruction targeted at novice writers, as well as automated tools to tailor feedback and scaffolding to individual students.

In addition to grounding their work in the writing research literature, designers of composition support tools will likely need to avail themselves of the full gamut of natural language processing techniques to analyze students' texts with regard to syntax, semantics, and discourse. However, in texts produced by novice writers, grammatical errors and incoherent discourse abound, which may present serious challenges for natural language processing since the majority of current NLP tools have been developed for well-formed texts. While existing NLP tools have been successfully used in writing support systems designed for expert writers (Mahlow and Piotrowski, 2009), common structural issues in novice compositions are likely to prove problematic for current tools. However, recent work has begun to explore techniques for handling ill-formed texts that are similar to those produced by novice writers. For example, Gamon et al. conducted a word-level analysis of texts written by non-native English speakers (2008). Focusing on two types of errors (determiners and prepositions), they use decision-tree

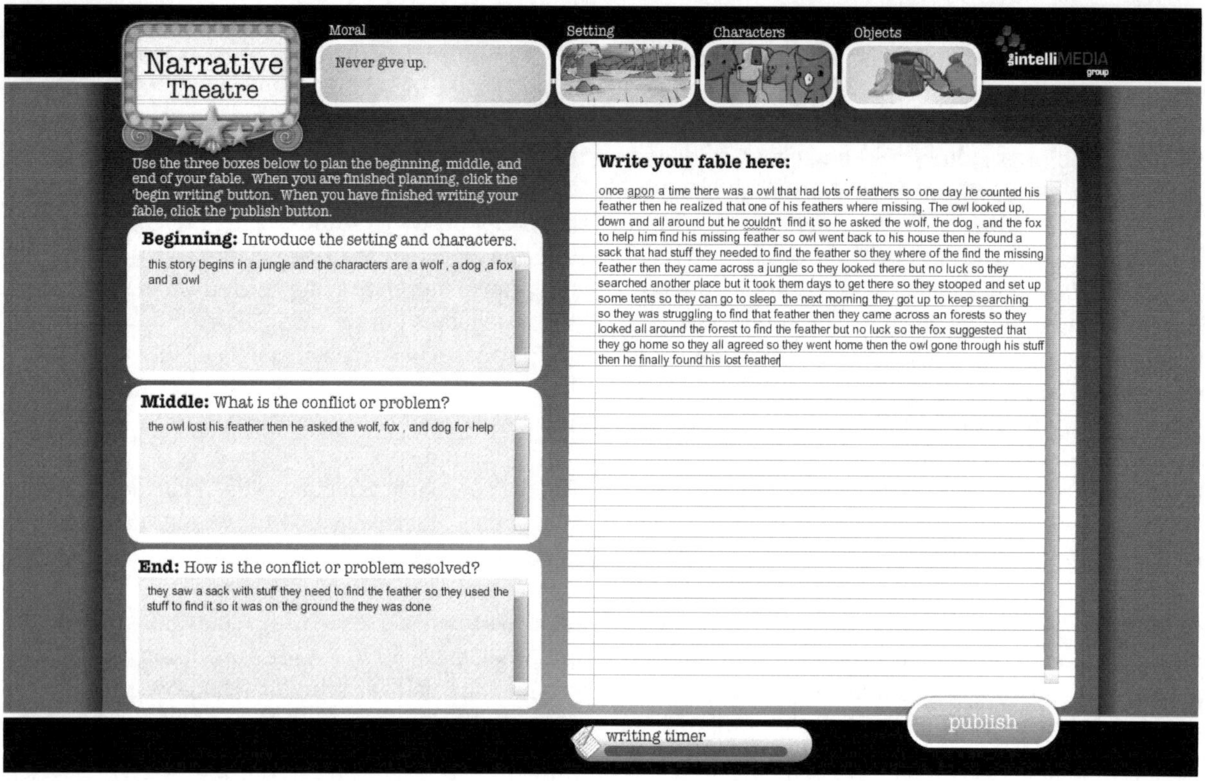

Figure 1. Narrative Theatre fable composition support environment.

classifiers in combination with a language model trained on a large English corpus to detect and correct erroneous selection of words. Wagner et al. investigated the detection of grammatical malformedness of individual sentences (2007). They found it effective to combine a shallow approach that uses *n*-grams and a deep approach that uses syntactic parse results. Higgins et al. explored the overall coherence of texts written by students (2004). Using support vector machines, their system identified the portions of text that resulted in coherence breakdowns with regard to relatedness to the essay question and relatedness between discourse elements.

To date, a relatively small number of intelligent tutoring systems have been developed to support student learning in the language arts, and even fewer have sought to specifically address writing. Sourcer's Apprentice is a web-based learning environment to help high school students gather, evaluate, and integrate information for writing essays about history topics (Britt et al., 2004), although Sourcer's Apprentice did not seek to apply NLP tools to understand or scaffold students' compositions directly. Other work on intelligent tutoring for language arts, such as Project LISTEN (Mostow and Aist, 2001) and REAP (Heilman et al., 2007), has addressed vocabulary learning and reading comprehension.

3 Narrative Corpus Acquisition

To investigate narrative composition in novice writers, a study was conducted with more than one hundred middle grade students using a narrative composition support environment. The NARRATIVE THEATRE (Figure 1) is an interactive environment designed to capture both the process and products of writing.[1] Targeting a user population of sixth grade students (age typically 12 years) and the genre of fables, the NARRATIVE THEATRE enables students to create stories in an environment that was specifically designed to scaffold novices' composition activities during a timed story plan-

[1] The version of the NARRATIVE THEATRE used in the study reported in this paper is the forerunner of a more general creativity support environment. It is under development in our laboratory that will employ NLP techniques and intelligent graphics generation. The study reported here was conducted to inform the design of the creativity enhancement environment and intelligent tutoring systems to support composition.

ning and writing process. The NARRATIVE THEATRE employs a multimedia interface created with Adobe's Flash® development platform and AIR runtime environment. Its design was inspired by a worksheet that is widely used as part of the Grade 6 writing curriculum.

During the planning phase, students select a moral, a setting, a cast of characters, and a set of objects for the story they will create. The system provides nine different morals, four settings, ten characters, and twenty objects from which students may choose. Each setting is accompanied by a visual representation, which can be enlarged by clicking on the image to highlight salient features of the setting. Characters and objects are also visually represented by static graphics, which were designed to be neutral in gender and expression in order to allow students creative choice when filling narrative roles with the characters.

Once the choices have been made, students are presented with a screen that allows them to view their planning decisions and begin structuring their fable. The planning area allows students to make notes about what they would like to have happen during the beginning, middle, and ending. The top of the page contains windows that display the setting, characters, and objects that were chosen earlier, and that can provide more information via a mouseover. Students craft a plan for the beginning (setting and characters are introduced), middle (conflict and problem), and end (conflict resolution) of their stories. For each of the three major segments of the story, they formulate a textual plan. After the planning information is entered, the students may begin writing (Figure 1). They then create the actual prose, which is entered as raw text. The writing and revision phase are supported with a spell-correction facility. All student activities including interface selections and the text streams from planning and writing are logged and time-stamped.

During the study, a total of 127 sixth-grade middle school students (67 males, 60 females) participated in the study. The students ranged in age from 10 to 13. Approximately 38% of the students were Caucasian, 27% African-American, 17% Hispanic or Latino, 6% Asian, 2% American Indian, and the remaining 10% were of mixed or other descent. Students participated as part of their Language Arts class. The study spanned two days for each student involved. On the first day, the students were seated at a computer and asked to fill out a pre-experiment questionnaire, which required approximately twenty minutes. On the second day, the students were again assigned to a computer. They were presented with the NARRATIVE THEATRE interface, which asked them to enter a unique identification number. Once correctly entered, the students were presented with a short instructional video that described the features and operation of the interface. They were given fifteen minutes to complete the planning activity, which included choosing a setting, main characters, props, and deciding the beginning, middle, and end of their story. Once planning was completed, or time ran out, the students were given another thirty-five minutes to write their fable. After their fable was completed, the students were asked to complete a post-experiment questionnaire. This survey was also allotted twenty minutes for completion. In total, the study lasted ninety minutes.

4 Findings

Three categories of analyses were performed on the NARRATIVE THEATRE corpus: an analysis of natural language processing tool performance (specifically, an analysis of syntactic parsers), an analysis of coherence and cohesion in the written texts using the automated cohesion metric tool Coh-Metrix (Graesser et al., 2004), and an analysis of students' writing processes.

As part of an investigation of students' individual differences in writing, students' language arts skills were measured by their scores from the prior year's End-of-Grade reading test. Subjective ratings of writing ability were also obtained for each student from their teachers. The reading scores were used in the presented analyses because they were obtained through systematic testing, but it is interesting to note that the objective reading scores and subjective writing scores were found to be strongly correlated by calculating the Spearman's correlation coefficient[2], $rho = .798, p < .0001$. The high correlation suggests that reading scores can serve as a reasonable indicator of language arts skills.

[2] Spearman's correlation coefficient was used because of the ordinal nature of the reading and writing measures (Myers and Well, 2003).

Coh-Metrix feature	Below-Grade	At-Grade	Above-Grade	F(2, 110) =
Hypernym, nouns	5.9 (0.93)	6.17 (0.81)	6.53 (0.43)	1.24 Below-Above**
Hypernym, verbs	1.44 (0.18)	1.49 (0.18)	1.48 (0.17)	3.72
Causal cohesion	0.83 (0.09)	0.87 (0.1)	0.39 (0.16)	3.70 Below-Above** At-Above**
LSA, paragraph to paragraph	0.34 (0.19)	0.45 (0.22)	0.49 (0.18)	3.89 Below-Above** Below-At*
LSA, sentence to sentence	0.21 (0.14)	0.24 (0.11)	0.22 (0.09)	0.48
Personal pronoun usage	107 (35.88)	101 (29.98)	89 (19.37)	2.25 Below-Above*
Pronoun to noun phrase ratio	0.36 (0.12)	0.35 (0.10)	0.30 (0.06)	2.21

Table 1. The effects of reading grade-level on select Coh-Metrix features. * denotes $p < .1$ and ** denotes $p < .05$

4.1 Natural Language Processing

Two syntactic parsing tools were used to analyze students' fables and develop an initial account of the performance of current natural language processing tools on a corpus of novice-generated narrative texts. The Link Grammar Parser (Temperley, 1995) and Stanford Parser (Klein and Manning, 2003) were run on the entire corpus, and their performance recorded.

Link parsing provides insight into the number of grammatically malformed sentences observed in each fable. Link grammars center on the notion of linkable entities directly combined with one another, as opposed to tree-like structures. Link parsers attempt to identify one or more syntactically valid representations, where each entity is paired with another. Passages were split into sentences using OpenNLP, and then run against the Link Grammar Parser (Temperley, 1995). If a sentence had no suitable link based on the parser (e.g., "Last dog I saw a great movie"), it was considered "broken" because it lacked an appropriate linkage. A ratio of sentences without appropriate linkage to total sentence count was used to characterize the link parser's performance on each student's fable.

On average, the Link Grammar Parser found linkages for 41% of sentences (SD=.22). Interestingly, reading level was shown to have a marginal effect on the link parser's success rate, $F(2,110) = 5.78$, $p = .06$. Post hoc Tukey's tests revealed that above-grade level readers were marginally more likely to write linkable sentences than at-grade level readers, $p = .07$. The effect was strongly significant between above-grade level readers and below-grade level readers, $p = .003$.

The Stanford parser was used to investigate the frequency with which sentences could be successfully parsed. A parsing failure was noted any time the tool was forced to fall back to a PCFG parse. On average, the Stanford parser produced a parse for 91% of students' sentences. A significant effect of reading grade-level on Stanford parser success rate was observed, $F(2,110) = 4.41$, $p = .015$. Post hoc tests showed that above-grade level readers wrote significantly more sentences that could be parsed than below-grade level readers, $p = .02$. There was also a marginal difference observed between below-grade level readers and at-grade level readers, $p = .08$.

Gender was not found to have an effect on the percentage of linkable sentences, nor the number of Stanford parser failures.

4.2 Individual Differences and Written Texts

Several analyses were conducted to investigate individual differences in students' written texts. Analyses focused on writing length, cohesion characteristics, coherence characteristics, and spelling errors. Fable lengths were measured in characters ($M = 1346$, $SD = 601$).

A marginal effect of reading grade-level on fable length was observed, $F(2,110) = 2.89$, $p = .06$. Post hoc tests showed that at-grade level readers tended to write longer fables than below-grade level readers, $p = .10$. Gender was also found to have a significant effect on writing length. Specifically, females tended to write longer fables than males, $F(1,110) = 4.41$, $p = .04$.

Writing process feature	Below-Grade	At-Grade	Above-Grade	F(2, 110) =
Avg length of deletion, planning	21.30 (8.31)	28.18 (11.14)	30.99 (12.37)	8.34 Below-Above*** Below-At***
Avg length of deletion, writing	23.42 (9.26)	27.74 (10.28)	33.06 (16.80)	5.18 Below-Above***
Mouseovers/min	0.19 (0.15)	0.09 (0.07)	0.07 (0.05)	11.81 Below-Above*** Below-At***
5+ second revision count, planning	9.14 (6.62)	5.43 (4.43)	2.37 (2.36)	12.70 Below-Above*** Below-At*** At-Above*
5+ second revision count, writing	18.04 (7.84)	14.21 (7.81)	13.37 (7.52)	3.83 Below-Above* Below-At*

Table 2. The effects of reading grade-level on writing process characteristics.
* denotes $p < .1$, ** denotes $p < .05$, and *** denotes $p < .01$.

To investigate cohesion and coherence in students' fables, the corpus was analyzed with Coh-Metrix, a tool for analyzing the cohesion, language, and readability of texts (Graesser et al., 2004). At the core of Coh-Metrix is a lexical analyzer, syntactic parser, part-of-speech tagger, and reference corpora (for LSA) that processes text and returns linguistic and discourse related features. Coh-Metrix measures several types of cohesion, as well as concreteness, connectives, diversity in language, and syntactic complexity. Concreteness is measured using the hypernym depth values retrieved from the WordNet lexical taxonomy, and averaged across noun and verb categories.

Results from an analysis of reading grade-levels and Coh-Metrix features are presented in Table 1. Interestingly, above-grade level students were observed to have lower causal cohesion scores than at-grade level or below-grade level students. The converse is found in an examination of paragraph-to-paragraph LSA scores, which are often used to measure semantic cohesion. Below-grade level readers tended to have lower semantic cohesion scores than at-grade level readers. LSA scores on adjacent sentences and all combinations of sentences were not significant across any of the groups. Sentence-to-sentence LSA scores were also not significant across groups.

Gender did not have a significant effect on causal cohesion, hypernym depth of verbs, or paragraph-to-paragraph LSA values. However, gender was found to have a significant effect on hypernym depth of nouns, $F(1,110) = 15.96$, $p = .0001$. Males tended to use more concrete nouns in their writing passages, with an average difference of .6 in hypernym depth. The ratio of pronouns to noun phrases was also significant between genders, $F(1,110) = 10.19$, $p = .002$. Females had a 38% pronoun to NP ratio whereas males were at 32%. Gender had a significant effect on sentence-to-sentence LSA scores, $F(1,110) = 19.9$, $p = .0001$. Males tended to have a higher LSA score across adjacent sentences ($M = .27$, $SD = .11$) than females ($M = .18$, $SD = .1$). Finally, gender had a significant effect on personal pronoun incidence score, $F(1,110) = 9.12$, $p = .003$. Females used personal pronouns as 11.1% of their content whereas males used them as 9.3% of their content.

An examination of the number of spelling errors remaining in student fables, as well as students' usage of the built-in spelling corrector, was conducted. However, no significant effects were observed across reading level or gender.

4.3 Individual Differences and Writing Processes

Several features in the student interaction logs were chosen to investigate key aspects of students' writing processes. Specifically, these features include planning length, planning and writing time, revision behavior, pauses in text production, and reviews of prior planning decisions.

On average, students spent 665 seconds planning their fables and 2199 seconds writing their fables ($SD = 535$). Students also typed 537 characters on average while planning their fables ($SD = 254$). No significant effect of reading level was observed on planning length, but reading level did have a significant effect on time spent in the planning phase, $F(2,110) = 12.76$, $p < .0001$. Below-grade level readers spent significantly more time on planning than at-grade level readers, $p = .001$, as well as above-grade level readers, $p < .0001$. There were also significant differences in writing time across reading level groups, $F(2, 110) = 6.47$, $p = .002$. Below-grade level readers took significantly more time composing their fables than at-grade level readers, $p = .05$. Also, below-grade level readers took significantly more time to write their fables than above-grade level readers, $p = .003$.

Females tended to write longer passages in the planning section than males $F(1,110) = 4.68$, $p = .03$. Time spent on the planning section was lower among females than males, $F(1,110) = 3.92$, $p = .05$. Females also spent less time on the writing section than males, $F(1,110) = 3.87$, $p = .05$.

Students' revision behaviors were gauged using a heuristic that measures edit distances between successive snapshots of fables collected at one-minute intervals during composition. Each minute, a static snapshot of student's fable progress was taken and logged. Edit distances between successive snapshots of students' fables were measured using the Google Diff, Match and Patch tools to make "before" and "after" comparisons (Google, 2009). Comparing two successive snapshots of a single fable, a revision was defined as any insertion of text that occurred before the tail end of the fable.

The effects of reading level on revision in both the planning and writing stages is presented in Table 2. During the writing stage, a significant effect of grade-level was observed on average revision length between below-grade level readers and at-grade level readers, as well as between below-grade level readers and above-grade level readers. Within the planning section, at-grade level readers revised more text than below-grade level readers, and above-grade level readers revised more text than at-grade level readers. Self-efficacy for writing was found to be significantly correlated with average revision length in both the planning, $r = .21$, $p = .03$, and writing, $r = .31$, $p = .001$, stages.

Pauses between successive keystrokes were investigated during both the planning and writing stages of NARRATIVE THEATRE interactions. For the purpose of this work, a pause is defined as a keystroke made five or more seconds after the preceding keystroke. Keystroke pauses were categorized as either an appendage or a revision, depending on whether they occurred before the tail end of the passage (revision) or after the tail end (appendage). For the planning section, below-grade readers paused significantly more often than at-grade readers. Also, at-grade readers paused before revising significantly more often than above-grade readers. The effects of reading level on a number of writing process subscores are shown in Table 2.

Gender had a significant effect on pauses prior to revision in the writing phase, $F(1,110) = 3.26$, $p = .07$. Females paused on more occasions than males. However, no gender effect was found for pause behavior during the planning phase.

During the planning and writing stages of NARRATIVE THEATRE interactions, students could review their prior planning selections—including characters, objects, and settings—by hovering the mouse over the respective region near the top of the screen (mouseover). Upon hovering the mouse over the appropriate region, a graphical illustration of the student's planning selection was presented. Mouseover instances were recorded to obtain insight into idea generation, or instances where the student was contemplating what to write next. Mouseovers were calculated in terms of average mouseovers over time (in minutes). The effects of reading ability on mouseover behaviors are shown in Table 2.

For the mouseover metric, reading level had a significant effect on the mouseover rate. Below-grade level learners tended to use the mouseover feature on a more frequent basis than both at-grade level and above-grade level readers. There was not a significant difference between at-grade level and above-grade level groups.

The effect of gender on mouseover rate was significant, $F(1,110) = 9.93$, $p = .002$. Males used the mouseover feature on fewer occasions than females.

5 Discussion

The performance of the two parsers differed widely. The Stanford Parser was able to parse over 90% of fables, but the Link Grammar Parser was only successful for about 40% of the fables. While parser failure is not always indicative of poor grammaticality, every sentence that failed on the Stanford Parser contained either misspelled words or run-on sentences. Many of these were indicated by errors in the sentence segmentation as well.

There were also indications that students' language arts skills may influence the grammaticality of their written sentences; significant effects of reading level were found on both the Stanford Parser's success rate and the Link parser's success rate. The fact that below-grade level students constituted a considerable proportion of the study's student population suggests that pedagogical writing support tools should be capable of handling the variations inherent in students' writings, and leverage natural language processing results to inform tutorial feedback.

Paragraph-to-paragraph LSA scores tended to increase with reading level. This has implications for semantic cohesion (Graessar, 2004) and indicates that students with a higher reading assessment score produce stories that satisfy this particular dimension of cohesion. However, the converse was true for the Coh-Metrix measure of causal cohesion, where above-grade level students actually produced the lowest cohesion scores. One possible explanation could stem from differences in vocabulary skills between above- and below-grade level students; students who exercise a larger vocabulary may be penalized by Coh-Metrix's cohesion metric. Alternatively, the result may be related to the fact that below-grade level students tend to produce less text (Graessar, 2004). Clearly, students' individual differences in language arts ability affect the cohesiveness of the texts they write, but additional investigation is necessary to develop a clear understanding of the relationship between cohesion and language arts ability, as well as the implications for tailoring tutoring.

With regard to the writing process, the average length per revision was significantly greater for students of higher reading skill-levels. There is a possibility that this may be associated with more elaborate revision processes, which requires further investigation. It should be noted that the revision finding was more salient for the planning stage of NARRATIVE THEATRE interactions. This result may also indicate that below-grade level readers were somewhat less thorough when planning their fables. Further, differences in mouseover behavior were found across reading levels, apparently indicating a decline in the rate of mouseovers as reading level increased. This finding may be the result of below-grade level students experiencing difficulties in idea generation, or a lack of motivation. Finally, the number of pauses prior to revision was found to decrease as reading level increased. This result may point to difficulties with text production for lower language arts skill students. Difficulty translating ideas into text may point to a need for intelligent writing tutors to help reduce lower reading level students' cognitive load during writing.

6 Conclusions and Future Work

We have presented a study conducted with middle grade students to investigate the process and products of writing in a narrative composition support environment. The study found significant variations in syntactic parser performance associated with students' language arts abilities, as well as relationships between students' reading level and the grammaticality of their writing. For example, the stories of below-grade readers had a lower level of semantic cohesion than at-grade level readers, but surprisingly, above-grade level students' writings exhibited lower causal cohesion than both at-grade and below-grade level students. Reading level had a significant effect on time spent in the planning phase, and below-grade level readers spent more time composing fables than at-grade level readers. There were also gender differences, with females spending less time in both the planning and writing phases. There were also differences with respect to revision, with above-grade readers revising more than below-grade readers.

The study highlights important issues about how to design composition support tools. Composition support tools that are sensitive to students' individual writing abilities seem likely to be most effective. Natural language processing is critical for analyzing students' texts and informing the content of adaptive tutorial feedback. Intelligent writing tutors should utilize natural language processing techniques that can robustly handle the variations in students' writings, and deliver tailored scaffolding informed by analyses of students' texts and writing processes.

The findings suggest that several directions exist for future work. Additional analysis is necessary to investigate the correctness of syntactic parses. Further investigation of students' individual differences in writing at the discourse and narrative levels is also necessary. Results from these analyses should then be used to inform the design of techniques for adaptive tutorial feedback in narrative composition support environments.

Acknowledgements

The authors wish to thank members of the North Carolina State University IntelliMedia Group for their assistance with the NARRATIVE THEATRE. This research was supported by the National Science Foundation under Grant IIS-0757535. Any opinions, findings, and conclusions or recommendations expressed in this material are those of the authors and do not necessarily reflect the views of the National Science Foundation.

References

C. Bereiter and M. Scardamalia. 1987. *The Psychology of Written Composition*. Lawrence Erlbaum Associates, Hillsdale, NJ.

V. W. Berninger, K. Vaughan, R. D. Abbott, K. Begay, K. B. Coleman, G. Curtain, J. M. Hawkins, and S. Graham. 2002. Teaching spelling and composition alone and together: Implications for the simple view of writing. *Journal of Educational Psychology*, 94(2):291–304.

M. A. Britt, P. Wiemer-Hasting, A. Larson, and C. Perfetti. 2004. Automated feedback on source citation in essay writing. *International Journal of Artificial Intelligence in Education*, 14(3–4):359–374.

C. A. Cameron and B. Moshenko. 1996. Elicitation of knowledge transformational reports while children write narratives. *Canadian Journal of Behavioural Science*, 28(4):271–280.

L. J. C. DeGroff. 1987. The influence of prior knowledge on writing, conferencing, and revising. *Elementary School Journal*, 88(2):105–118.

L. Flower and J. Hayes. 1981. A cognitive process theory of writing. *College Composition and Communication*, 32(4):365–387.

D. Galbraith, J. Hallam, T. Olive, and N. Le Bigot. 2009. The role of different components of working memory in writing. In *Proceedings of Annual Conference of the Cognitive Science Society*, Amsterdam, The Netherlands.

M. Gamon, J. Gao, C. Brockett, A. Klementiev, W. B. Dolan, D. Belenko, and L. Vanderwende. 2008. Using contextual speller techniques and language modeling for ESL error correction. In *Proceedings of the International Joint Conference on Natural Language Processing*, pages 449–456, Hyderabad, India.

Google Diff Match and Patch [Software]. Available from http://code.google.com/p/google-diff-match-patch/

A. C. Graesser, D. S. McNamara, M. M. Louwerse, and Z. Cai. 2004. Coh-Metrix: Analysis of text on cohesion and language. *Behavior Research Methods Instruments and Computers*, 36(2):193–202.

S. Graham. 2006. Strategy instruction and the teaching of writing: A meta-analysis. In C. A. MacArthur, S. Graham, and J. Fitzgerald, editors, *Handbook of writing research*. Guilford Press, New York, NY, pages 187–207.

S. Graham, K. R. Harris, and B. F. Chorzempa. 2002. Contribution of spelling instruction to the spelling, writing, and reading of poor spellers. *Journal of Educational Psychology*, 94(4):669–686.

J. Hayes. 1996. A new framework for understanding cognition and affect in writing. In C. M. Levy and S. Ransdell, editors, *The Science of Writing: Theories, Methods, Individual Differences, and Applications*. Lawrence Erbaum Associates, Mahwah, NJ, pages 1–28.

M. Heilman, K. Collins-Thompson, J. Callan, and M. Eskenazi. 2007. Combining lexical and grammtical features to improve readability measures for first and second language texts. In *Proceedings of Human Language Technology Conference*, pages 460–467, Rochester, NY.

D. Higgins, J. Bustein, D. Marcu, and C. Gentile. 2004. Evaluating multiple aspects of coherence in student essays. In *Proceedings of Human Language Technology conference/North American chapter of the Association for Computational Linguistics*, pages 185–192, Boston, MA.

J. A. Langer. 1985. Children's sense of genre: A study of performance on parallel reading and writing Tasks. *Written Communication*, 2(2):157–187.

C. Mahlow and M. Piotrowski. 2009. LingURed: Language-aware editing functions based on NLP resources. In *Proceedings of International Multiconference on Computer Science and Information Technology*, pages 243–250, Mragowo, Poland.

D. McCutchen, M. Francis, and S. Kerr. 1997. Revising for meaning: Effects of knowledge and strategy. *Journal of Educational Psychology*, 89(4):667–676.

J. Mostow and G. Aist. 2001. Evaluating tutors that listen: an overview of project LISTEN. In K. Forbus and P. Feltovich, editors, *Smart Machines in Education*. MIT Press, Cambridge, MA, USA, pages 169–234.

J. Myers and A. Well. 2003. *Research Design and Statistical Analysis*. Erlbaum, Mahwah, NJ.

K. VanLehn. 2006. The behavior of tutoring systems. *International Journal of Artificial Intelligence in Education*, 16(3):227–265.

J. Wagner, J. Foster, and J. Van Genabith. 2007. A comparative evaluation of deep and shallow approaches to the automatic detection of common grammatical errors. In *Proceedings of 2007 Joint Conference on Empirical Methods in Natural Language Processing and Computational Natural Language Learning*, pages 112–121, Prague, Czech Republic.

The Linguistics of Readability: The Next Step for Word Processing

Neil Newbold
University of Surrey
Guildford
Surrey, GU2 7XH, UK
n.newbold@surrey.ac.uk

Lee Gillam
University of Surrey
Guildford
Surrey, GU2 7XH, UK
l.gillam@surrey.ac.uk

Abstract

In this paper, we present a new approach to writing tools that extends beyond the rudimentary spelling and grammar checking to the content of the writing itself. Linguistic methods have long been used to detect familiar lexical patterns in the text to aid automatic summarization and translation of documents. We apply these methods to determine the quality of the text and implement new techniques for measuring readability and providing feedback to authors on how to improve the quality of their documents. We take an extended view of readability that considers text cohesion, propositional density, and word familiarity. We provide simple feedback to the user detailing the most and least readable sentences, the sentences most densely packed with information and the most cohesive words in their document. Commonly used verbose words and phrases in the text, as identified by The Plain English Campaign, can be replaced with user-selected replacements. Our techniques were implemented as a free download extension to the Open Office word processor generating 6,500 downloads to date.

1 Introduction

Spell and grammar checking have become inherent tools in many modern word processors even if their results are not always deemed appropriate. Work on writing tools has largely focused on improving these services, with superior grammar checkers being the emphasis of this work. However, there has been little effort on providing a deeper analysis of the text, such as covering its semantic content and its potential success in conveying the authors intended message to the reader. Research on readability aimed to provide an indication of the proportion of the population could understand the text but has been limited to simple checks of word and sentence length providing only some degree of feedback on where and why text is difficult to understand. Writing tools such as 'Stylewriter' scores documents based on average sentence length, number of passive verbs and overall style. The style analysis uses an indexes check for a wide variety of common editorial issues like jargon, hyphenation, sexist writing, clichés, grammar, redundancies and troublesome words which are either abstract, complex, misused or overused. However, their approach is based on a simple lookup of common writing patterns with no analysis of overall message clarity. More robust tools such as 'Coh-Metrix' (Graesser et al., 2004) deliver a substantial analysis but can leave casual users confused with the quantity of numerical data produced.

In this paper, we discuss how linguistic techniques have been deployed to measure largely ignored aspects of the text, which can benefit authors when writing texts. We use automatic summarization techniques to measure how cohesive or consistent the text is and parts of speech patterns to identify multi-word expressions, which indicate portions of text densely, packed with information. We also deploy corpus linguistics methods to measure the familiarity of words in everyday use. These techniques expand upon readability research to provide a series of tools for authors giving pointers to where their documents might confuse their intended audience.

Proceedings of the NAACL HLT 2010 Workshop on Computational Linguistics and Writing, pages 65–72,
Los Angeles, California, June 2010.

2 Background

In principle, readability measures identify some proportion of the population who could comfortably read a text. Historically, readability research has focused primarily on producing a numeric evaluation of style of writing to associate textual content to a particular rating or the level of education of readers. Readability research largely traces its origins to an initial study by Kitson (1921) who demonstrated tangible differences in sentence lengths and word lengths, measured in syllables, between two newspapers and two magazines. Kitson's work led variously to the development of readability metrics, many of which are available in certain software applications. Further discussion of these formulae can be found elsewhere (Dubay, 2004). More recent considerations of readability account for reader factors, which consider certain abilities of the reader, and text factors, which consider the formulation of the text (Oakland and Lane, 2004). Reader factors include the person's ability to read fluently, level of prior subject knowledge, lexical knowledge or familiarity with the language, and motivation and engagement. Text factors account to some extent for current readability metrics, but also cover considerations of syntax, lexical selection, idea density, and cognitive load. Oakland and Lane's view of readability suggest that it may be possible to generically measure the difficulty of text as an artifact, but that "text difficulty" necessitates consideration of each reader. Our work elaborates that of Oakland and Lane in identifying difficulties in the apparently neat separation of the factors. In this section, we propose a new framework for readability that builds on Oakland and Lane by making consideration of the relationship between text, reader, and author. We explore, subsequently, how word processors might use such a framework to help authors get across their intended messages.

2.1 Matching Text to Readers

In writing a document, an author has to be mindful of the needs of his anticipated audience, particularly if they are to continue reading. There must be some correlation across three principal aspects of a text: the nature and extent of its subject matter, its use of language, and its logical or narrative structure. The audience can be defined by their degree of interest in the subject, how much they already know about it, their reading ability, and their general intelligence. If the author needs to learn more about a set of potential readers, standardized tests are available to measure levels of intelligence and reading skill, while interest and prior knowledge can be assessed by ad hoc surveys.

Two kinds of measure are suited to appraising text structure: logical coherence and propositional density. By logical coherence, we mean the extent to which one statement is ordered according to a chain of reasoning, a sequence or chain of events, a hierarchy or a classificatory system. By propositional density we mean the closeness, measured by intervening words, between one crucial idea and the next. The less coherently ordered are it's the ideas and the greater their density, the larger the cognitive load on the reader.

If characteristics of the audience have been ascertained, the author must ensure that what he is writing is generally suitable for them. A readability formula will produce a quick check on a given text for an author, and comparisons have been made amongst measures to correlate with specific human performances over largely disjoint sets of texts. For our current considerations, we are interested in providing more useful feedback to the author that a single numerical value. A readability analysis should be able to provide hints to the author on how to improve their text. However, this is not to say that existing measures are adequate, we propose other elements of text that can be measured instead of, or in addition to those examined by the currently established readability formulae. Our new framework for readability, describing the factors to be considered is presented in Fig. 1. The matches needed for easy reading describes how an author can match their text to their target audience. In the remainder of this section, we elaborate these factors.

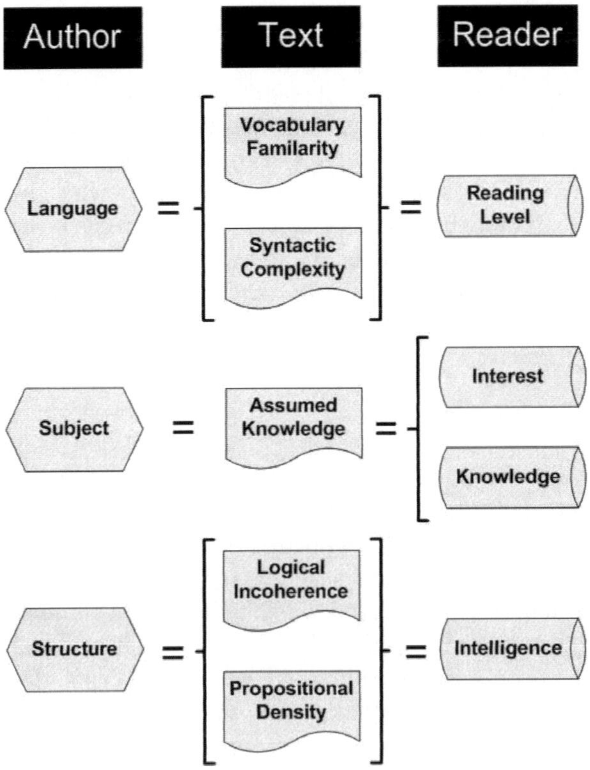

Figure 1: Matches needed for easy reading

2.2 Language

When matching text to reader, the author needs to consider the level of language and style of writing. This can be described as the vocabulary familiarity and syntactic complexity of the writing. These aspects are generally measured by the existing readability formulas as word length and sentence length. Readability metrics generally determine the difficulty of a word by counting characters or syllables. However, Oakland and Lane suggest that word difficulty can be determined by examining whether the word is challenging, unusual or technical, and cite word familiarity as more effective means of measuring word difficulty. The process by which readers develop word familiarity is through their language acquisition and the development of their language capability. Frequency plays an important role in building knowledge of a language so that it is sufficient to understand its written content. Diessel (2007) showed that linguistic expressions stored in a person's memory are reinforced by frequency so that the language user expects a particular word or word category to appear with a linguistic expression. These linguistic expectations help comprehension.

Frequency was also found to be fundamental in reading fluency as words are only analyzed when they cannot be read from memory as sight words. A limited knowledge of words affects reading fluency as readers are likely to dwell over unfamiliar words or grammatical constructions. This impedes the reader's ability to construct an ongoing interpretation of the text. The reading fluency of the reader is dependent on their familiarity with language. When readers find text populated with unfamiliar words it becomes harder for them to read. This is especially prevalent in scientific or technical documents where anyone unfamiliar with the terminology would find the document hard to understand. The terminological nature of specialized documents means that terms will appear with disproportionate frequently throughout the documents in contrast to what one would expect to encounter in everyday language. Terminology extraction techniques exploit this relationship to identify terms. We adapt this method by contrasting word frequency within documents with familiarity in general language. We determine the difficulty of a word by its familiarity.

Vocabulary does not tend to exist in isolation. The vocabulary may be well-defined, yet included in overly verbose sentences. Consider these two sentences:

1. "We endeavor to maintain the spinning of all the plates."
2. "We try to keep all the plates spinning."

The first sentence uses passive voice, the second uses active voice. Writing guidelines, such as those presented by the Plain English Campaign (1979), often recommend active voice wherever possible. Active voice uses fewer words and helps readers build a mental representation of the text. Existing readability formulae consider that long and complex sentences can confuse the reader and whilst we support this view, we consider that each individual sentence should be scored to allow the author to identify the particularly troublesome sections of their text. When matching text to reader, syntactic complexity should be examined not just for the entire document but whether each sentence is appropriate for the reading level.

2.3 Subject

To learn from text, a reader needs to associate the new information to their existing knowledge. This task can be helped by the reader's interest level. Kintsch et al. (1975) showed that we find stories easier to remember than technical texts because they are about human goals and actions, something to which we can all generally relate. Scientific and technical texts require specific knowledge that is often uncommon, making the texts impenetrable to those outside the domain. This suggests that readability is not merely an artifact of text with different readers having contrasting views of difficulty on the same piece of text. Familiarity with certain words depends on experience: a difficult word for a novice is not always the same as a difficult word for an expert. Reader characteristics such as motivation and knowledge may amplify or negate problems with difficult text. When matching text to reader, the author needs to consider the target audience and the extent of their knowledge.

Many readability metrics do not make distinctions based on the background knowledge of the reader. As discussed in relation to vocabulary, word familiarity can give a better indication of word difficulty than word length. A longer word may only be difficult for a particular reader if unfamiliar, and certain shorter words may even be more difficult to understand. Consider a general reader confronted in text discussing a 'muon': This short term would be rated as simple by current readability formulae. However, a majority of people would be unfamiliar with this term, and only physicists are likely to know more about the term, its definition, and related items. One way to measure background knowledge would be to consider the extent of use of known terms in the text with direct consideration of previous documents within the reader's experience.

Entin and Klare (1985) showed that more readable text is beneficial for those with less knowledge and interest. In their study, students were presented with written material below their reading level. When the reader's interest was high, text below their grade level did not improve comprehension. However, when the reader's interest was low their comprehension was improved by simpler text. This suggests that more readable text improves comprehension for those less interested in the subject matter. We consider the need to capture and analyze the user's experience with prior documents as a proxy for reader knowledge and motivation. Given a reading history for a user, we might next build their personalized vocabulary with frequency information, and therefore measure familiarity with words on an individual basis. In the same way that an expert is familiar with the terminology of their subject, we can reflect the background knowledge required by a reader to interpret the text correctly. When matching text to reader, word difficulty should be measured, if the information is available, on an individual basis.

2.4 Structure

Well-written text requires a structure that readers can readily use to find the information they need and to understand it correctly. Text can become confusing when information is inappropriately presented. Most sentences, when taken out of context, can become multiply ambiguous. When we read text, we build a collection of the concepts described within it. We identify these concepts with words and phrases using pragmatic, semantic, and syntactic features. We build certain interpretations with these blocks of words that tend not to combine randomly or freely, but rather they keep preferred company (Firth, 1957). These collocations are evidence of preference for certain friends, and these friends may be kept at certain distances. For example, words impose restrictions over synonyms, excluding some from their group of friends so that 'strong tea' may be acceptable, but 'powerful tea' may not. A reader unfamiliar with such constructions might not understand the precise meanings or variations. In addition, individual words may not be particularly difficult but their combination may produce different meanings to the component words. Collocation statistics may indicate compound nouns with specialized meaning but increased likelihood of misinterpretation. Consider, for example, 'glass crack growth rate': each word should be relatively easy to understand, but interpretations due to bracketing (Pustejovsky et al., 1994) might lead to interpretations of a 'crack growth rate' made of 'glass', and an unpacking of semantics may be useful in removing ambiguities due to bracketing.

Most researchers agree that collocations are sequences of words that co-occur more often than by chance, with certain assumptions of randomness, and can be found using statistical measures of association. Some linguists consider collocations are the building blocks of language, with the whole collocation being stronger than the sum of its parts. They describe collocations as lexical items that represent uniquely identifiable concepts or semantic units. Smadja (1993) elaborated criteria for a collocation, describing them as recurring and cohesive domain-dependent lexical structures such as 'stock market' and 'interest rate', and suggested how components can imply collocations, for example 'United' produces an expectation of 'Kingdom', 'Nations', or 'States'. When frequently combined linguistic expressions develop into a processing unit, many of the linguistic elements are ignored and the whole chunk is compressed and treated as one semantic unit. These units often develop into terms with multiword units representing singular concepts. This relates back to the assumed knowledge of the reader. However, for readers unfamiliar with the terms, we have identified two methods called 'Propositional Density' and 'Lexical Incoherence' for processing semantic units.

When a significant amount of information is conveyed in a relatively small amount of text, the reader can become confused. We identify this problem as 'Propositional Density'. Although long collocations form semantic units that reduce conceptual complexity, problems occur when numerous semantic units are described within a short space of each other causing the reader to make numerous inferences. The number of ideas expressed in the text contributes to the work required of the reader to interpret the text correctly. Propositional density may be measurable by examining the quantity of objects within short distances of each other. These objects can be labeled with single nouns or multi-word expressions. By measuring the number of unique semantic units, we can approximate the workload required for processing or interpreting the text correctly.

The second problem with text structure is called 'Lexical Incoherence' and occurs when writers present new information to the reader without making clear its relationship to previous information. The writer assumes that they have provided enough information to allow readers to follow their arguments logically. Repetition of concepts, terms, and other referents provides a structure for the reader to connect with. It is through this repetition that a series of links can be made between the sentences. There is a relationship here to work on lexical cohesion (Hoey, 1991). If a large number of new, seemingly unrelated ideas are being introduced, low cohesion would be expected and measurable. Efficiency can be increased here by using synonyms. Semantic units can be referred to by a number of different labels and by identifying these different labels we can more accurately find the prominent ideas in the text.

3 Open Office Readability Report

To implement our new techniques for measuring readability, we used OpenOffice.org 3, which is the leading open-source office software suite. As it can be downloaded and used free of charge, it has an already established user base and allows third-party developers to write extensions for their applications. These extensions are made available to download for any OpenOffice.org user. We created the readability report extension for 'Writer', the open office word processor, to implement our readability techniques. The extension generates 5 separate components devised from our framework for readability incorporating the matches for easy reading. The components analyze the text factors in the framework to provide an indication of the corresponding reader factor. The author can use this information to help match their text to their audience. Each author and reader element is addressed by a component as follows:

- Language -> Reading Level
    - Weirdness Measure
    - SimpleText SmartTags
- Subject -> Interest and Knowledge
    - Not yet implemented
- Structure -> Intelligence
    - Propositional Density
    - Lexical Coherence

The two language components address both the text features of vocabulary familiarity and syntactic complexity. We have yet to implement a component to assess the subject of the text. The separate components, which consist of either a generated report or text annotation through SmartTags, are detailed in the remainder of this section.

3.1 Weirdness Measure

The first generated report uses our new readability formula based on word frequency. Unlike the established readability formulas, our measure can be applied to an individual sentence, allowing the report to highlight the most and least readable sentences in the document. We use frequency information from the 100 million word tokens of the British National Corpus (BNC) to act as a reference corpus. The frequency counts for each word along with the number of words in the sentence are used to determine the sentence readability. The score for the document can then be ascertained as an average value for each sentence. We use log and other arbitrary values to bring the final number into a similar range as the other readability formulas.

$$2.1 \times \ln(n_{SL} \sum \sqrt{\frac{f_{SL} n_{GL}}{(1 + f_{GL}) n_{SL}}}) \quad (1)$$

Eqn. 1 sentence-based familiarity
f is word frequency, n is word count at sentence level (SL) or corpus level (GL).

Based on research by Stuart et al., (2004) concerning the frequency of use of apostrophes by children, contractions such as "n't" and "'s" were considered as separate words with their difficulty determined by their frequency count as per any other word. This method for analyzing contractions generated more effective results from the BNC.

In addition, to the weirdness measure the report provided the scores from the established readability formulas, 'Flesch Easy Reading', 'Flesch Kincaid', 'FOG', 'SMOG' and 'ARI'. To help authors understand the significance of the readability values, a series of ratings were provided for each measure (inc. Weirdness), which grade a document as either 'Simple', Easy', 'Good', 'Challenging' or 'Difficult' using a series of threshold values.

3.2 SimpleText SmartTags

SmartTags were developed in Open Office to highlight sections of documents and add contextual information. The readability report extension uses SmartTags to highlight difficult words and phrases in the text, as identified by http://www.plainenglish.co.uk/. The 'SimpleText SmartTags' provide suitable alternatives for these phrases which can be inserted automatically into the text. The user can click on the SmartTags and select a possible alternative from a list of suitable replacements. These SmartTags help authors avoid using common, verbose expressions that hinder the clarity of their writing. Gillam and Newbold (2007) showed that plain English substitutions can lower readability scores.

3.3 Propositional Density

To measure the structure of the text, we use an analysis of propositional density. This report analyses how many concepts and ideas are referred too in the text and was entitled the 'Brain Overload Report' to make it more accessible to the users. An expert in a particular subject will often use specific terms and jargon resulting in too much information being presented to the reader within a short space. This can lead to learners become fatigued and confused. The report measured the amount of single and compound nouns in comparison to the length of the sentence in which they occurred. Sentences with contained a large amount of 'glue' words, such as 'the', 'at', etc. would score lower than sentences loaded with multi-word expressions. The score for the document is determined as an average value for each sentence. For user convenience, we use some arbitrary values to bring the final number into a similar range as other readability formulas.

$$2n \frac{u + n}{3(n - c)} \quad (2)$$

Eqn. 2 sentence-based propositional density
u is the number of semantic units, n is sentence length, c is the number of collocated words.

Whilst this report was devised to measure the structure of the text, there is an also an element of subject which determines the assumed knowledge of the reader. Scientific and technical texts often require specific knowledge represented in the text through frequent use of terminology. The single and multi-word terms increase the propositional density of the document indicating that the text will be difficult for novices in the subject matter. Texts intended for a general audience should score low on propositional density. As with the previous report, the resulting score is graded as either 'General', 'Introductory', 'Scholarly', 'Technical' or 'Specialized' to help authors understand the impact their text will have on their intended audience.

For further feedback, the most frequent multi-word expressions are listed to show authors which expressions are contributing the most to their score. Each expression is unpacked into its component expressions and a frequency count throughout the document is taken for each. The most frequent component expression is then used as a basis for unpacking the full expression. For example, 'current account balance' will be unpacked into either 'balance of current account' or 'account balance which is current', depending on which of the component expressions, 'current account' and 'account balance' are more frequent. If a suitable component expression is found, the full unpacked expression is suggested to the user as a possible way of rewriting the collocation. The separating glue words are selected depending on the Part-Of-Speech tagging of the concluding phrase in the rewritten expression.

3.4 Cohesion Measure

The 'Cohesion Report' uses techniques for automatic summarization to measure how easy a document is to follow. It identifies the lexical words in each sentence and uses them to recognize sentence bonds. Hoey (1991) described a sentence bond as two sentences sharing 3 or more lexical words. The score for a document is determined by the number of sentence bonds against the total number of possible sentence bonds.

$$\frac{b}{s(s-1)} \qquad (3)$$

Eqn. 3 document-based lexical coherence
b is the number of sentence bonds, s is the number of sentences.

The sentence with the highest number of bonds is highlighted in the report as the most representative of the document. For further feedback, the report shows the words that are the strongest themes in the text. These are lexical words that were used the most often to create sentence bonds. By increasing the references to these themes the author can improve the cohesion of their text. Authors need to pay particular attention to sentences with no sentence bonds are these are adding nothing to the coherence of the text. These can be seen by using the detailed report described in the next section. The cohesion measure is primarily useful for documents about a specific subject; fictional writing will often score low for cohesion. As with previous reports, a document will be graded as either 'Creative', 'Digressing', 'Consistent', 'Coherent', or 'Fluent'.

3.5 Detailed Report

An option is provided for a detailed report that allows authors to view the readability score of each sentence in their document. The report is displayed in a spreadsheet and shows the results of each of the established readability measures and the new scores discussed in this paper. The spreadsheet can be used to identify the most troublesome sentence in the document. This is particularly useful for examining the results of the cohesion measure, as sentences that are not adding to the cohesion of a document can be easily identified.

4 Conclusion

The weirdness measure correlates with the other readability formulas that have been shown to indicate the required reading age of the text, when analyzing a large range of texts. Our results show that frequency is a good indicator of word difficulty. Table 1 shows a sample of texts, ordered by increasing difficulty, ranging from children's books to technical reports and the correlation of the weirdness measure to the established formulas. For sentences, containing relatively long but commonly used words such as 'information' and 'business', the score calculates more probable figures than the established readability formulas. Certain children's books (for example "Jabberwocky") contained made-up or nonsense words which caused the measure to the rate the texts as difficult. It should be noted that the other readability formulas rated these texts as simple. We consider that these types of text would be confusing to non-native speakers of the language, with the effect of these words, which are unique to the document, being the same as terminology.

Text	Weird	Kincaid	FOG	SMOG	ARI
Lucky	8.54	3.80	5.26	6.74	2.75
The Absolutely True Diary	9.40	4.62	6.31	7.05	3.33
Coraline	9.41	5.08	7.24	8.05	4.41
Associated Press, Fed Revises	11.78	10.92	12.50	11.96	11.20
Bloomberg, U.S. Leading Indicators	11.76	11.28	13.33	12.60	11.51
USA Today, Greenspan predicts	12.07	11.36	13.25	11.21	12.27
Greenspan, to congressional committee 2005	12.75	14.32	16.29	14.60	14.55
Greenspan, speech 2005	12.52	15.69	17.80	15.70	16.18
Bernanke, speech 2008	13.29	16.28	17.97	15.58	17.72
Bernanke, report to congress	13.24	16.60	18.80	16.31	17.80
Correlation		**0.98**	**0.98**	**0.96**	**0.99**

Table 1: Correlation of weirdness measure with established readability formulas

Currently, we have not implemented a means to measure the user's experience with prior documents as a proxy for reader knowledge and motivation. In future, we would build a personalized vocabulary for each user with frequency information, and therefore measure familiarity with words on an individual basis. At present the Open Office extension is more useful for writing general texts as opposed to specialized or technical documents. Certain elements such as the weirdness measure and the SimpleText SmartTags become less useful with more expert texts and the prevailing use of terminology. Other aspects such as propositional density and lexical coherence are of less use when analyzing children's books. This style of writing can score high for propositional density due to extravagant character names (e.g., "The Mad Hatter" and "Cheshire Cat") increasing the number of compound nouns. Lexical cohesion is also low for any fictional writing.

We are looking at improving the lexical cohesion measure with the consideration of synonyms. Semantic units can be referred to by a number of different labels and by identifying these synonyms; we can more accurately identify the prominent ideas in the text. It is the repetition of terms and their synonyms, along with other referents that provide a structure for the reader to connect with.

The extension was made available on the Open Office website in July 2009. In six months the extension had received over 6,500 downloads indicating, along with positive user feedback that demand for word processors to go beyond simple spelling and grammar checking of text and provide more feedback is considerable.

References

H. Diessel. 2007. Frequency effects in language acquisition language use, and diachronic change. *New Ideas in Psychology*, 25(2):108–127.

W. H. DuBay. 2004. *The Principles of Readability*. Costa Mesa, CA: Impact Information.

E. B. Entin, G. R. Klare. 1985. Relationships of measures of interest, prior knowledge, and readability comprehension of expository passages. *Advances in reading/language research*, 3: 9–38.

J. R. Firth. 1957. *Papers in Linguistics: 1934-1951*. London, Oxford University Press.

L. Gillam, and N. Newbold. 2007. *Quality assessment. Deliverable 1.3 of EU eContent project LIRICS*, URL:http://lirics.loria.fr/doc_pub/T1.3Deliverable.final.2.pdf, last accessed 28 February 2010.

A. C. Graesser, D. S. McNamara, M. M. Louwerse, and Z. Cai. 2004. Coh-Metrix: *Analysis of text on cohesion and language. Behavior Research Methods, Instruments, and Computers*, 36:193–202.

M. Hoey. 1991. *Patterns of Lexis in Text*. Oxford, OUP.

W. Kintsch, E. Kozminsky, W. J. Streby, G. McKoon, and J.M. Keenan. 1975. Comprehension and recall as a function of content variables. *Journal of Verbal Learning and Verbal Behavior*, 14:196–214.

H. D. Kitson. 1921. *The mind of the buyer*. New York, Macmillan.

T. Oakland and H. B. Lane. 2004. Language, reading, and readability formulas: Implications for developing and adapting tests. *International Journal of Testing*, 4(3):239–252.

The Plain English Campaign. Established 1979. URL:http://www.plainenglish.co.uk/, last accessed 28 February 2010.

J. Pustejovsky, S. Bergler, P. Anick. 1994. Lexical semantic techniques for corpus analysis. *Computational Linguistics*, 19(2):331–358.

F. Smadja. 1993. Retrieving collocations from text: Xtract. *Computational Linguistics*, 19(1):143–178.

M. Stuart, M. Dixon, and J. Masterson. 2004. Use of apostrophes by six to nine year old children. *Education Psychology*, 24(3): 251–261.

Author Index